THE LITTLE]

BIG MIRACLES

True Tales from Granddad's Rocking Chair

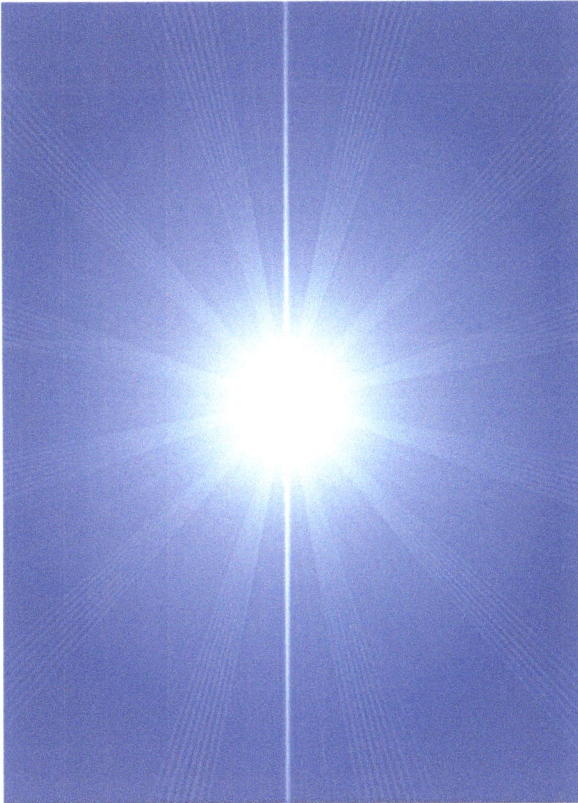

Alan D Edmondson

Alan D Edmondson

Kingdom Publishers

www.kingdompublishers.co.uk

The Little Book of Big Miracles
Copyright© Alan D. Edmondson 2023

ISBN: 978-1-911697-71-8

1st Edition 2023 by Kingdom Publishers
London, UK.
You can purchase copies of this book from any leading bookstore or email
contact@kingdompublishers.co.uk

REVIEW

"In his eminently easy-to-read and often hilarious style, Alan shares how God has, in one way or another, been very involved in His life.

This book will show you just what it means to be a Christian. That is, not someone who goes to church and performs their rites and rituals, but someone who experiences God in all kinds of ways on a daily basis.

From miracles of healing to a change of character; from brushes with death to finding the right direction in a career, Alan shares what to most of us are the ordinary experiences of life. What do you do when you are given a cancer diagnosis? How do you cope with suffering? With losing a loved one?

Alan relates many stories from his life how God has helped him through these and many other situations, often supernaturally.

If you are a Christian you will be encouraged by how much God wants to be involved in every tiny detail of your life. Your faith will be built up as you read.

If you are not a Christian, or even a sceptic or a doubter, there is much here that will convince you that God loves you and cares for every detail of your life. This little book will show you how real miracles can be a part of your life, too."

Rev. Mark Lindsell (Baptist Minister)

"I found this book very different in its presentation, which made it easy to read, comical in the pictures it created in my mind at times, yet powerful in what it was saying about life's ups and downs and the relevance the writer's faith in the Lord Jesus played in the experiences he faced.

The short chapters dealing with real life experience will make it very readable to those who don't find reading books easy.

Life wasn't easy for Alan at times and that's what made it real and relevant for me."

Canon Max Wigley
Archbishops College of Evangelists

" 'An everyday story of country folk' was the sub-title of a popular radio programme, some years ago, implying that, even for country folk, everyday life could be far more interesting and eventful than we might think.

Some people have skewed ideas about Christians, that they are boring, legalistic, straight-laced and humourless. Alan would not be my friend if he was like that!

A wonderful American Christian leader, founder of the Vineyard Church, John Wimber, said, "God's people do God's stuff, and on the way miracles happen!" That is, genuine Christians, who regularly read the Bible, pray, worship and serve God in their everyday lives, expecting to see God at work, do, from time to time, witness miracles!

Alan is such a Christian. He is not a vicar/minister/pastor, missionary, or 'professional' Christian. For most of his professional life he was an accountant, and latterly, he and his wife, Maria, ran a small care home.

Alan is serious and thoughtful about things that matter, but has a ready smile, sharp wit, lovely sense of the ridiculous, and is good company.

I do hope you will enjoy and be encouraged and challenged by his, 'Little Book of Big Miracles'.

Rev Chris Murray (Anglican Vicar)

Dedication

I dedicate this Little Book of Big Miracles to my wife, Maria, who has shared much of what is here, our two sons, and our grandchildren - by bloodline, by marriage, and by being chosen by them.

Contents

THE LITTLE BOOK OF BIG MIRACLES

True Tales from Granddad's Rocking Chair

"We will tell the next generation the praiseworthy deeds of the Lord, His power, and the wonders He has done." Psalm 78 v 4.

DEAR READER

This is the story of God's goodness to an ordinary man, whose life has been full of mistakes, and still is whilst on this earth, but to whom God has extended His love, compassion, and forgiveness.

This is not because of any goodness on my part, but because of God's goodness.

My prayer for you all is that it will inspire you to see beyond the apparent "luck" and "coincidences" of life to a God who loves you. A God Who wants you to see that His hand is outstretched towards you. That He cares for you. That He wants you to get to know Him.

All these events really took place. They are not fanciful tales as some might like to persuade you. If you look for them, you too can see His hand on your life, just as I have seen His hand on my life.

May the God of all Peace bring you His Word of Love, Salvation, and Truth to dwell in your innermost being. May His Peace and your Contentment in Him bear Good Fruit to the Glory of His Name, and be your Salvation for ever.

With lashings of love to all who read this.

Alan D Edmondson

Granddad, husband, dad, and so many other relational titles too long to list!

December 2023

Chapter 1
A LITTLE INTRODUCTION
(or, What's it all about then?)

I always like books that have **little** introductions, don't you? If they are pages and pages I think, "This could have been included as Chapter One, and then I would have read it and not skipped it".

Or some of them are so long they could have been a book in themselves, a sort of Volume 1. So here goes with my **little** Introduction, as Chapter One, just to be on the safe side. So .....let's go ....

Now, you will more than likely be one of three types of person.

Firstly, the kind of person who believes in lucky coincidences and chance and Lady Luck, and that when good or bad things happen that's just how life goes. I hope that what you read here will give you a different way of looking at life. But, if not, that you will enjoy reading about some of the strange things that have happened to me in my life; that you will chuckle at the funny side of many of them, and be touched by those that have a little sadness to them. I do, of course, tell them from my point of view, but I am sure you will enjoy them just the same.

Or, secondly, you may be the totally opposite kind of person. Someone who is totally convinced that there are no lucky coincidences in life. Someone who believes that God has your life in His hands; and that, whatever happens, good or bad, nothing can separate you from His love. I hope that what you read here will encourage you to trust Him even more.

Or, thirdly, you may be the sort of person who comes with an open mind. Someone who is not afraid to change your ideas about things when the evidence is there. May this collection of real life events be helpful to you in considering whether life is all about "luck" and "bad luck", or whether there is indeed a "Someone Who Loves You"; a Someone who has your best interests at heart, and who wants you to know Him as your best friend.

I have tried to make it fun to read just as a collection of some of the experiences of my life. But from my point of view this book is about God, not me. It is about a loving God who has intervened in my life in many ways, and who has given me many true tales to tell.

There are many other stories I could tell. This book is more like a short introduction to the faithfulness and goodness of God in my life. How God has supported, strengthened and encouraged me during the sometimes seriously difficult times, particularly those times when I have had no strength of my own left in me.

I have also enjoyed some really good times. I might get round to writing about them one day. You never know.

So – I hope that you will catch something of the nature of this loving God from these true tales. God yearns for each one of us to welcome Him in to our everyday life, so that He can make our life on this earth full of meaning. More importantly, so that He can give us a future with Him, our loving God, that will never end.

The choice most definitely is ours. He won't force Himself on us. He loves us too much to take away the gift of choice that He has given to us.

I hope and pray that it will draw you close to The One Who loves you, and Who wants you to know Him really well.

May God's Blessing and Peace enfold you in His arms as you read.

Alan D Edmondson

Granddad, husband, dad, and many other relational names.

December 2023

"I will remember the deeds of the Lord, …. you are the God who performs miracles, You display Your power among the peoples."
Psalm 77 vv 11a & 14

Chapter 2
THE TROUBLE WITH SHINGLE
(or, How I nearly didn't get to write this book Part 1.)

I don't know now exactly how old I was when this happened, but I know that my younger brother was four or five years old; so that would make me seven or eight. How life can be changed by a single event. There are people alive today who wouldn't be had God not intervened.

Mum, dad, my younger brother and I, an aunt, and an uncle, went to the seaside.

Reaching the beach, we stopped, and our family began a deep discussion about something or other, although I noticed that our aunt was keeping an eye on us.

It was boring stuff for us two youngsters, so we sneaked off to dip our toes in the sea. This was much more exciting.

It was a shingly beach, and if you know anything about shingly beaches you may guess what happened next?

The breeze was cold, the sun shone, and the waves washed up the sloping beach, and then drained back through the shingle with a pleasant tinkling sound.

It all looked very friendly and cheerful.

The sea looked so exciting and fun that we went to the very edge of the dry shingle. At least, I stopped there, sensing that the sea may not be so friendly and cheerful on a sloping shingly beach as it might appear.

"Don't go any further," I warned my younger brother.

But you know what younger brothers are when their older brother tells them not to do something. They give you a funny look and then do precisely what you've told them not to do.

Being the adventurous sort, Colin stepped towards the incoming wave to experience the pleasure of the sea stroking his ankles and toes. His face brightened in a big smile. As the wave started to recede he suddenly realised what an astonishingly brave move this was, and his smile changed to fear.

15

I somehow sensed what was coming next and stepped forward onto the wet shingle and grabbed his wrist.

The next instant he was dragged off his feet. The shingle gave way beneath our feet, and we slid down towards the sea. It had suddenly lost its friendly look and was glaring fearsomely at us, intent on swallowing us up. How treacherous can you be!

Fear filled my heart.

Keeping my grip desperately tight on Colin's wrist, I turned and started running up the beach. At least I tried to.

I felt like Alice in "Alice Through the Looking Glass". My feet were pounding away trying to run up the beach, out of harm's way, but all that was happening was that the shingle just fled away as quickly from beneath my feet. I was running like I was trying to win the one hundred metres Olympic event, but not moving!

I made my legs go faster and faster, my heart pounding, my lungs working like crazy, but the shingle continued to fly away from beneath my feet. I was running as fast as I could just to stand still, with the sea snapping at our heels.

My brother was being bounced about by the waves like a ping pong ball on a stormy sea, and I was hanging on to him for dear life, literally so, desperate not to have my hold on his wrist broken.

Meanwhile our family was still calmly chatting contentedly away, oblivious to the drama unfolding behind them. More importantly our aunt had turned away to take a closer part in the conversation just as I started to need her, desperately need her.

A thought flashed through my mind, "If you let go you might save yourself".

A second thought flashed through my mind, "But you would live in misery for the rest of your life, abandoning your precious brother in his time of dire need."

A decision flashed through my mind, "We are going to live together or die together".

It probably took less than a second for all three thoughts to chase each other through my brain.

My grip tightened.

You know, on a cold deserted beach, in the offseason, you wouldn't expect to see a couple arrive and then disappear within a few moments. Or maybe it does happen.

"Sorry love but the wind's too chilly for a picnic on the beach," or,

"Gosh I've left the frying pan on. Best go home," or,

"You forgot the barbecue? How are we going to do the pig roast?"

But that is just what happened. The moment we two started battling with the sea and the shingle, fighting to stay alive, just such a couple turned up.

It seemed a long time before the man in the party saw that we needed help. He raced over, grabbed my hand, and with a great effort pulled us both up the beach and out of harms way. I have learned since that in desperate situations time stretches out, and in reality it may have been just a few seconds.

I was so exhausted and frightened that I couldn't speak, and was not able to thank him. But the couple walked off as if they had done nothing.

Then my family looked round, and we all went back to the car.

They were all totally unaware that their names came close to appearing in the local paper that week, describing how their four sons halved in number that day, as the bodies of their two youngest were found on a beach, several miles down the coast.

I never did tell them.

So that's Part 1 of how I nearly didn't get to write this book, the first of a few.

Some might say that this was total coincidence, and we were just lucky. And if this was the only true story I had to tell about "coincidences" and "luck" then it might be easy to believe that.

But when "coincidences" and "luck" pile up? We-e-ell, you may understand why I think that "Someone Important and Powerful" is looking after me.

And so, let's read on.

Psalm 94 verse 17. "Unless the Lord had given me help, I would soon have dwelt in the silence of death."

17

Chapter 3
MORE FUN THAN WALKING ON WATER
(or, An Uplifting Experience)

By the time I was nine I didn't believe in God. No, really.

I couldn't touch Him, see Him, smell Him, hear Him, taste Him (See Psalm 34 v 8 below!), so He couldn't possibly exist, right? Logical eh? I didn't need to write a book about it, like Richard Dawkins, to convince myself I must be right. It was too simple an equation for that. For the mathematicians among you

[No (T+Se+Sm+H+T)] = No God (QED).

Right?

I didn't know, when I was nine, that, when you work things out logically, the information you start with has to be true, otherwise your conclusions are total nonsense. In my early days of trying to learn computer language I was taught "Rubbish in = Rubbish out". And it still applies!

For example, if you start with the idea that our Sun revolves around the earth – which is what some people once thought, and got upset with Copernicus for telling them that God created planet Earth to revolve around our sun – then you could conclude that we are at the centre of the universe, instead of what we are. The truth is, we are a tiny little speck in an obscure part of the Milky Way Galaxy. But a very important speck, of course.

I had Christian parents who made me go to Sunday School, and one fine day a Children's Evangelist came to talk to us.

He made it clear that God's message to us humans is very simple.

Firstly God has given us an important gift. It is the gift of being able to choose what we believe, and what we do with our lives. They both have consequences. One good, the other remarkably awful.

He said that the most important choice we make is between (1) believing what God says about Jesus, and (2) not believing what God says about Jesus.

Firstly we can choose to trust in Jesus for the forgiveness of the wrong things we have done in our life. The consequence of this is that we will live for ever with this loving God in His wonderful and amazing world – that's right, it is a wonderful place, *(see "Steps to Heaven")*, and it never *stops*.

Secondly, we can choose that we don't, or won't, believe what God says about Jesus. The consequence of this choice is that we go to somewhere where God isn't, and life is going to be hell – that's right, it's an awful place, and it never *stops*.

"Jesus said, 'There is no middle way or alternative'," he told us."That is it! Heaven or Hell as a final and permanent destination for your soul. and you get to choose which one you go to."

By the way, we are souls with bodies, not bodies with souls, so whatever happens to your body your soul lives on – somewhere. Make sure it's in a nice place, which is what this is all about.

I wasn't sure I believed in heaven or hell, or God for that matter; but I thought that if hell did exist it wasn't going to be a lot of fun. No Kids Holiday Club or Butlins holiday camp, or gobstoppers or chewing gum, you might say.

I said, "God, if you do exist you must be able to do anything. So if you do exist, please forgive me for asking this, but make me walk home on air like that man said. If I do, I will know that you are real, and I will accept You into my life for ever. I really mean it".

Some people say it's amazing what our imaginations can tell us, if we wish for it enough. Only one snag with this miracle; I didn't wish for it. But neither did I say it couldn't happen. I just waited to see. I was totally open to it happening or not happening, a bit like a scientist carrying out an experiment to see if his theory is true.

I thought, "If God really exists He can do what this man says He can do. If He doesn't exist .... well.... I haven't lost anything. But if God does exist, and I refuse to surrender my life to Him, I am in more trouble than I could ever be with my mum and dad, and the trouble never ends."

It was a "no-brainer" as they say.

So there I was, walking home down Pipers Hill Lane in Kettering as if on air!

I experimentally stamped my foot on the ground – twice – and felt .... Nothing!

I seemed as tall as the street lamps.

And then I saw a man coming up on the other side of the road, looking thoughtfully across to my side of the road. Whoops!

I thought, "I hope he doesn't see me up here. He'll have the shock of his life! And I'll feel so embarrassed".

My body and mind were feeling a lightness I had never experienced before in my nine years of life.

I arrived home, stepped through the door into the hall, and ..... felt the floor under my feet!

I thought "That was fantastic", as you would, and went outside to repeat the experience.

But God had said "Yes" to me walking home on air, not floating about for the rest of my life, making people nervous.

That night I asked God for a repeat performance, but God isn't into sensationalism. He's into saving people from the consequences of their sins.

"The wages of sin is death", He tells us, "but the Gift of God is eternal life through Jesus Christ our Lord". (See Romans Chapter 6 verse 23.)

But, - and this is really important - if we ask Jesus for His forgiveness, and ask Him to change us for the better, He will nail all our sins to His cross. He will add them to the sins of hundreds of millions of other people who have also asked Him for His forgiveness. When we leave this planet Earth, we will meet up with the countless other people who have made Him Lord of their lives, and who, when they leave this earth, will live with Him for ever.

You will probably guess correctly why I have never looked back.

Hell is more than scary!

It's the pits.

Psalm 34 verse 8. *"Taste and see that the Lord is good; blessed is the man who takes refuge in Him."*

Chapter 4
THE WATERY GRAVE
(or, How I nearly Exploded.)

The thing about deciding to follow God when you are a small child is that you accept Him into your life with the understanding of a small child; which is a good thing according to Jesus. But when you get older you are able to think things through a bit better and with more understanding and reason; which is just how it should be.

At sixteen I had been going, with my family, to one of our local Baptist Churches. You may know that Baptist churches baptise people who accept Jesus as Lord of their lives by immersing them fully in water.

At this age some stop believing what God says and start to believe what man says, which is what went wrong at the very beginning with Adam and Eve. They chose to believe Satan instead of God, and we have all been suffering ever since. Not God's fault then. Ours! And it continues to be, most definitely - Ours!

I had been to a lot of these baptismal services, and found them quite moving, as many people do today, Christians and non-Christians.

Then came the day when I was asked to move, not my emotions, but myself!

At the end of every Baptismal Service the minister always gave an invitation for people who wanted to be baptised to come forward to the front. So that day he gave the invitation as usual.

My younger brother went out like a shot, but me? We-e-ell, I was an extremely shy teenager who was petrified of standing in front of crowds.

I felt like I did when I was "The Hangman" in Sergeant Musgrave's Dance.

I had no words to say.

"Just stand there with a noose in your hands" was the simple direction.

I was shaking with more terror than the person I had come to hang! Not that I really did hang him you understand. It was a play after all.

So-o-o I didn't move. But I knew God wanted me to go out to the front with the others. So I started making excuses to God, pointing out that I was a very shy teenager, that I couldn't possibly go out in front of something like three hundred or so people, that I was already trembling at the idea like a leaf in a strong Autumn wind, and I'd look such a fool shivering away where everyone could see me.

I felt a pressure beginning to build up inside me. I knew what God wanted me to do, but I was resisting doing it. The pressure carried on building up inside me, as I carried on with my weak excuses, until it became so great I felt I was going to explode and make a mess of the balcony in my church!

At that point I said, "Alright God, alright, I give in. I will go out, but when the service is over. Not in front of everyone."

Immediately, two pictures appeared in my mind's eye, side by side.

On the left was a cylindrical black hole. Moving about within this deep and impossibly black hole were wispy shapes like coloured air; they looked like transparent heads. Each had a downturned mouth, and was very clearly in deep agony. The sense of desolation was overpowering, and left me more frightened than I had ever been before or have been since.

On the right was a line, which I knew was the time-line of my life. It was a bit like a graph, with hills and valleys. I knew that the hills were the difficult times of my life, and the valleys were when life was a bit easier.

There seemed to be a lot of steep hills, but as time went on they became smaller, until my life-line flattened out for a while, and then finished. The sense was that God would be with me during all these times, easy or difficult.

These were my choices.

Two choices.

The path of disobedience or the path of obedience.

Each had its own consequence.

THE LITTLE BOOK OF BIG MIRACLES

Disobedience led to never ending misery in this dark hole. Obedience led to a life where God would be with me all of the way to strengthen and support me, even though it would be really tough at times.

I don't remember my trip out to the front, but I know it was fast, and I do remember treading on my elder brother's toes as I pushed past him, much to his astonishment and pain.

We were, I think, about ten of us. Half of us were boys and half were girls. We came together once a week to be taught what it meant to be baptised. They wanted us to know for sure what we were committing ourselves to.

So, several weeks later we all sat at the front of the church robed in our "Baptismal Gowns" waiting to be baptised. The gowns were provided by the church and were different for men and women.

The girls had to be warned to wear something more than underwear underneath, as their white maidenly gowns became translucent when they got wet. I thought that was something they really needed to put right to spare the blushes of those maidens who had a short memory. One of them did forget, and we all blushed. The next baptismal service they had changed them for more modest ones.

We boys ... well ... I think the church must have found a job-lot of black serge gowns from a monastery that was closing down and got them at a knockdown price.

They reached to the floor and were heavy enough going into the water, but coming out of the water was a real struggle. Two deacons were strategically placed to pull us out, so that we didn't literally "die with Christ" in the baptismal pool!

I was ecstatic. My nervousness had totally disappeared. I felt a lightness within me that contrasted remarkably with the heaviness of my "Baptismal Gown".

So I didn't explode, and what died in the baptismal pool was my old nature, and I was raised to new life by the power of The Holy Spirit.

And after 79 years, yes, my life has had its troubles, but I've also had more settled and fun times. More importantly, God has been with me all these years as

He promised.

And no, I haven't been perfect, and, yes, I'm still "work in progress".

But, God has been perfect, and I wouldn't have done the things I've done, and lived the life I've lived, if I'd been disobedient and stayed in my seat – and maybe exploded there and then leaving an awful mess for the cleaner to clear up!

Jeremiah, Chapter 21: verse 8 "Thus says the Lord: See, I am setting before you the way of life and the way of death. Choose life."

Chapter 5
HOW I DIDN'T JOIN THE ARMY
(or, A narrow escape from being shot at for a living.)

It was one of those days when my work as an accountant was at its worst. The tedium of ticking figures (pounds, shillings, and pence in those days) from one set of hand-written accounting records to another meant that any other job in the whole wide world seemed livelier and much more fun; even washing up!

The person I was doing this mind numbing work with called for a break for lunch. Thankfully we went out for a breath of fresh air and a stroll, with the hope of finding a strengthening sandwich as a bonus.

As we walked along we came across an Army Recruitment Office. We paused and looked at each inquisitively.

"Do you fancy joining the army?"

I'm not sure who asked the question, but it was clearly in both our minds. Anything seemed better than sitting in a stuffy office using green pens (the audit colour for that year) to place a bored tick when the pounds, shillings, and pence in each book agreed, which they invariably did. What an achievement!

We pushed open the door. It gave a welcoming ping, and we stepped inside. To our right was a desk with an officer sitting behind it. We walked over, and, as we opened our mouths to explain what we were there for, he stood up and left without seeming to see us.

The only other officer was already talking to a possible recruit and was being very attentive to his questions. He totally ignored us. Maybe he hadn't been taught how to put customers at their ease, and keep them in the shop? So we politely waited.

Then we waited, and he carried on ignoring us. We waited some more, and he carried on with his new recruit, and ignored us. We checked our watches and waited, and waited. Then we looked at each other and waited, and continued not to receive the attention we deserved as potential soldiers of the Queen and defenders of the Realm.

One more look at our watches and lunch time was drawing to a close. So, in obedience to our contract of employment, which was quite clear on the matter, we decided we had better return to pick up our green pens and carry on decorating our client's beautifully kept ledgers with bored green ticks.

I don't recall now whether we managed to find a strengthening sandwich or went hungry, but I have since learnt that at that time army food was pretty monotonous, and needed Tabasco Sauce. Whether that was to kill germs, smother the flavour, or keep you on your toes, I'm not sure. I did try it once. One drop nearly burned my tongue off!

So we escaped all that because, by mutual unspoken understanding, we never darkened the doors of the Army Recruitment Office ever again, or thought an army life might be better than making not-so-artistic green marks on accounting records.

Green ticks might be boring, but green pens don't fire a slug at you and suddenly end your life, like a rifle does. And if, as a soldier, with the excuse of war, you fire at someone to show how good your training's been, they will more than likely fire back to show you how good their training's been.

I am not saying that being a soldier, or joining the Royal Navy, or the Royal Air Force, is wrong in itself. We need brave men and women who are prepared to live a dangerous life to defend our country. They are heroes. I am just saying that it was wrong for me.

You may be wondering where the miracle might be.

For me it was amazing that as we walked through the door of the recruitment office we seemed to have become totally invisible! Not for the first time in my life I had the sense that God intervened, and, in His wisdom, so distracted the Recruitment Officers that, in effect, they didn't notice us at all, and so saved us both from a very foolish off-the-cuff decision.

God's plan for me was not to be trained to take lives, but to be trained to save and heal lives, just like He does. He wanted, and wants, my heart to beat with His heart.

Incidentally, my idea of being on the front line was probably a bit of a young man's romantic dream. As an accountant I would probably have been put in the Pay Corps, and found it even more boring than splashing green ticks all over someone's carefully written accounting records!

Proverbs 19 verse 21: "Many are the plans in a man's heart, but it is the Lord's purpose that prevails."

Chapter 6
STEPS TO HEAVEN
(or, How I nearly didn't get to write this book Part 2.)

I came back to earth with a thud, and I felt scared; and then the prayer meeting started.

My mum and I were at our church for the Wednesday evening prayer meeting. Directly behind us a couple had been talking about an elderly gentleman who, at the meeting two or three weeks before, had passed away.

I was thinking to myself that it must have been amazing, talking to God one minute, and then, all of a sudden, there is Jesus with a huge smile on His face giving you a big hug and saying,

"Welcome! You're so special! I'm so glad you're here. This is heaven. Have fun. And by the way, the party's at seven this evening. Probably go on all night. See you later. Don't miss it." As if you would miss such a party!

Suddenly I was there! I was at the foot of a broad flight of steps, and beginning to walk up them. High above me were two golden gates, flung wide open. On each side were two shining angels, smiling in welcome and joy. With one hand they held on to the golden gatepost, and with the other they reached down to help me up the steps and through the dazzling gates.

A scintillating light such as I had never seen before shone through the gateway, and a hubbub of happy, joyful people reached me. I knew that if I got near enough to the top of the steps to see into this amazing place I would not be returning to planet earth. Then words came into my head.

"You can come in if you like Alan."

But I sensed the face of the One who spoke, and knew that He did not think that this would be my best choice.

"My mother," I cried out.

My dad had died just a few months before, and I thought that my mother would be devastated, losing her much loved husband, and then one of her four sons, so closely together,.

Immediately I was back in the prayer meeting, and afraid; but not by the prayer meeting. I had seen and sensed a place of unconditional joy, happiness, contentment, and peace, Peace with a capital P, where you lived without fear. A place where there is so much fun, happiness, and joy. In fact what most people long for.

And now?

Now I was back in a world of selfishness, criticism, lies, back biting, and evil intentions. A world where people cheat each other, kill, steal from each other, and they are unkind and unhelpful. Where there are wars, every kind of abuse, and where life is often tough, and we live with the question, "Who, who can I trust?"

One thing occurs to me. If I had died, I would have had an autopsy, and they would have found no earthly reason for my death.

I would have literally died for reasons that were out of this world!

Psalm 71 vv 14-15: "But as for me, I shall always have hope; I will praise you more and more. My mouth will tell of your righteousness, of your salvation all day long, though I know not its measure."

Chapter 7
THE CHRONICLE OF A "GOOD COMPANIONS MINOR"
(or, How I nearly didn't get to write this book Part 3.)

Some people are called "fey" because they sense things that other people don't pick up. However, being a Christian, I believe this is simply God telling us things about people and situations. When this involves people who love Him, He calls us to pray for those people, and into that situation. It often happens.

This true tale is about how God saved the lives of my elder brother and I, through our mother, 600 or so miles away.

Eric, my merchant naval brother, was back on leave. We decided to have a tour around the countries of Europe together for three weeks. This was before the Euro, so we had our pockets full of different currencies, trying to keep them separated from each other, which was quite tricky. It was also before free movement of people, apart from the Benelux Countries, so our passports were kept busy. None of which has anything to do with the story at all, but just gives you some sort of taste of the historical background.

I know you will ask, so, the Benelux Countries are Belgium (Be), the Netherlands (ne) (some call it Holland), and Luxemburg (lux), which gives us Be-ne-lux.

Being good scouts we packed camping and cooking gear, which we loaded into a blue Hillman Husky Estate. This we borrowed from our eldest brother John. Rather strangely the driving seat was angled slightly to the left. Again, this has nothing to do with the story, but I include it for those of you who like to know these things.

One evening we arrived in a small town. We found a grassy open space on the outskirts of it, and there pitched our tent, a Good Companions Minor. I was very proud of this tent, with its flysheet and sewn-in groundsheet, which was a new thing then.

We cooked our food, and, because of the cold, retired to the car to eat it. We turned the engine on to keep warm, read a bit, chatted a bit, and planned our route for the next day. We turned in early, closed up the tent and fell asleep.

600 miles away our mum woke up with a start. In her mind was a picture of her two sons coughing and choking in our tent. She started to pray to God for our safety.

In my Good Companions Minor, I woke up coughing and choking. This woke Eric, who started coughing and choking. A sense of supreme urgency came into my head. I had to get the tent flap open or we would not see morning. The Edmondson family would lose two of its four sons (sound familiar?).

I tried to bring my arm out of my sleeping bag but it felt as heavy as lead. Try as I might I couldn't move it. The sense of urgency was overwhelming, and I just willed my arm to move.

After what seemed an age, and with what seemed an effort as strong as Superman, I got my arm to move, and my hand to the zip on the flap. I dragged the zip up a few inches, and fresh air flooded into the tent which gave me strength to open the flap fully.

We both lay gasping in the fresh air, thanking God for the strength and determination He gave me to struggle against all odds, and overcome my weakness.

Our hearts slowed down, our breathing returned to normal, and I zipped up the tent again, leaving a couple of inches at the bottom. We turned over, fell asleep, and completely forgot about it.

Speculation is that the exhaust fumes from the car filled the tent, and, because of the sewn-in groundsheet, could not escape. My pride and joy had nearly killed us!

When we got home two weeks later mum gave me a quizzical look and tentatively asked if anything bad had happened to us whilst we were away. Strangely, I didn't immediately remember our near suffocation, and said,

"No. We were fine."

Eric glanced at me but made no comment. Mum looked a bit puzzled but said nothing more. But her puzzled expression made me think, and a few minutes later,

"Oh, yes ..." and told her our story.

It was then that she told us how God had woken her up in the middle of the night, 600 miles away, to pray for our safety, with a picture of us coughing and choking and near to death.

When we compared the date and the time, taking into account the different time zone, they matched exactly.

Psalm 91 vv 9-10: *"If you make the Most High your dwelling – even the Lord, who is my refuge – then no harm will befall you, no disaster will come near your tent."*

Chapter 8
MIRACLE ON DONOVAN AVENUE
(or, The Open Door of Opportunity.)

This is the romantic one!

I had learnt at the age of fourteen that women (that is, fellow teenagers) can look really smashing, then spoil it all by opening their mouths. I realised that I could make a disastrous mistake if I chose a young woman to be my wife on the basis of how fantastic she looked.

I asked God to please enable me to see beyond the physical appearance, and to see the personality. I asked Him not to let me marry anyone who was not His choice for me. Of course, it dawned on me later, that I had to be His choice for her, but I was still in my very selfish period of life.

And there she was! A vivacious and very personable young woman in her mid-20's, focussing on the dance steps of our tutor, at the famous "Court School of Dancing" in Wood Green, North London. Her attractive character poured out of every pore in her body. And she was pretty too!

I moved over to her at the mid-session break and introduced myself.

"I'm Douglas," I said.

I was using my middle name at this period of my life, thinking it really cool to do so. This led to an embarrassing admission later as you will find out.

"I'm Loulla. Are you Cypriot?"

Admittedly at that time I could be mistaken for one, but no, I was British, and proud of it to boot. My dad had always told us four sons of his that, "The British, The British, The British are best", after Flanders and Swan, and I was still believing it.

"Certainly not!" I replied with John Bull fervour.

Reflecting on this later I realised that this was not at all cool, and not to be recommended as a chat up line. It probably deserved a slap in the face, which, in those days, if you were an insulted lady, you could still give, without fear of being sued for assault.

But it didn't seem to annoy Loulla at all. She just kept on chatting away, as we swapped our reasons for being there.

I was there because I had recently discovered that I really liked dancing, and wanted to learn how to do it properly. My lovely companion was there because her mum, back home in Cyprus, had three young men waiting for her to look over, with a view to choosing one of them as her husband.

So, she wanted to be able to dance at her wedding.

This was quite strange in retrospect. Ballroom and Latin American dancing, which was what we were learning, bears little resemblance to the dancing of her village. In fact I challenge you to find any resemblance to the blend of Greek and Arabic dancing of her village, which can sometimes look more like a gymnastics display.

We liked dancing together, and became friends.

Then her cousin started coming to the lessons.

One evening I offered to drive Loulla home, and she accepted, but her cousin insisted on coming as well. This meant he had to nestle down on the back seat amongst my spade, fork, rake and hoe. I heard him utter a few "ouches" which I was really pleased about.

The back seat of my car, you see, was my mobile garden shed. At that time I was also learning how not to look after an allotment I rented, just off the North Circular Road in North London.

I dropped Loulla off, then her cousin at his place, and went home.

The next day I really wanted to see Loulla again, so after work I set off to see if I could find her.

Once I have driven down them, I have always been good at remembering routes. But, this was London, all twists and turns. However, I managed to puzzle my way through to a road I recognised. One of the roads on the right was the road in which Loulla lived. But which one was it?

I tried the second turning to the right, but very soon realised it was not the one.

I tried the next one.

This was more promising, but which was the house?

Half way down the road, on the left, a door opened, and a middle aged couple came out. They were talking to someone behind them, in the manner of people leaving after a visit. And then emerged …. yes, you're right, it was Loulla seeing them out, and bidding them goodbye.

I drew up at the kerb just as she was about to step back and close the door. The window, or in this case, the door of opportunity was about ten seconds, if that.

She saw me, paused, and welcomed me in to the Old People's Home where she lived and worked.

We saw more and more of each other over the next few weeks. I stayed longer and longer with her in the evenings, and my car became a virtual pumpkin. My landlady, Mrs Godfrey, warned me not to stay out past midnight, or she would lock the door and turn a deaf ear to my knocking! It was a close run thing on more than one occasion! But, if you've ever slept in a car seat, you will know how important it is to arrive at your lodgings before the front door is locked for the night!

After a few weeks I took her to see my mum. On the way we stopped for a cup of tea, and I decided that I had better tell Loulla that my family called me Alan. She still knew me as Douglas, and I didn't want her to arrive at my mum's to suddenly find out that everyone knew me by another name.

Loulla was very relieved at this, because at the time there was a TV programme with a character called Douglas who was a bit of a dimwit!

We were engaged shortly afterwards, much to her mother's annoyance. After all she had worked really hard to line these three possible husbands up ready for her to choose from when she arrived back home. In their village marriages were still being arranged. What! Choose your own husband? That just isn't done girl!

Eventually Loulla's mum was very thankful because I didn't know about dowries, and so didn't know to ask for one. And so she got away with giving us twenty silk and cotton sheets, and pinning a few hundred Cyprus Pounds on us when we danced later on. Not that I wanted a dowry. Just the youngest maiden of your family, thank you. I'm more than happy with her.

Incidentally those sheets are very precious. My mother in law had raised the silk worms from eggs, fed them on Mulberry leaves, unravelled the cocoons, spun the thread, and woven silk sheets on her loom. From the cotton grown on their farm she had spun the cotton into threads and woven cotton sheets on her loom. So we were given some of each, and we still have them.

We married in Loulla's village in Cyprus with much jubilation. Because weddings are a community event, almost everyone in the village turned out and joined in the celebration.

We are now known as Alan and Maria, and at the time of writing we have forty seven years of challenge and achievement together, our love for each other having been tested and tried to produce strength and resilience. Having stuck together through thick and thin we have a better and stronger love for each other than when we first fell for each other all those years ago.

I thank God for looking around the world and bringing us together from 2,000 miles apart and from two very different cultures.

When she was nineteen Maria was wondering whether to come to England to study. We found out that precisely during that time I had been moved to pray for my future wife on three occasions. I asked God to give her wisdom from Him on the decisions she should make for her future life. Thinking of praying a fourth time, I felt that a good decision had been made, and I didn't need to pray about it any more.

Proverbs 18 v 22; 31 v 30: *"He who finds a wife finds what is good, and receives favour from the Lord. A woman who fears the Lord is to be praised."*

The following is for the young at heart –

P.S. Actually, officially, we got married to each other twice!

"Wha-a-at! That's strange. How was that?"

You might well ask!

Well, we were told that there were two legal problems about getting married in Cyprus that could delay us there for weeks. To avoid all the fuss and bother, we were advised to get a marriage certificate in the UK before we went to Cyprus, although our real marriage was still to be in Maria's village church. That meant Maria could get a UK passport in her married name, and we could come back to the UK whenever we wanted.

So one lunchtime we went to the local Registry Office. Maria's employer, and a friend, came as witnesses, and all the legal forms were filled in, and signed off by us all. The Registrar then gave us our official UK Marriage Certificate. Job done!

But we didn't consider ourselves married yet; so Maria went back to work, and after work back to where she lived in the Old People's Home; and I went back to my work, and after work back to Palmers Green and my one room bedsit.

So that's why we celebrate our Wedding Anniversary when we got married properly at St George's, in Cyprus, which is the date inscribed on my wedding ring, but our UK Marriage Certificate has an earlier date.

Chapter 9
LITTLE BOY LOST
(or, A Nudge from Heaven.)

People were streaming towards me, and past me, as my eyes strained to pick out Andrew, just three years old, amongst the moving crowd. Deep dread and anxiety filled my mind. Where was he?

We had gone up to Birmingham to visit some nephews of Maria who were studying at the university there. We had decided to go for a walk in what became clear was a large and very popular park. As the saying goes, "All the world and his wife were there".

Suddenly Andrew was not with us.

I shouted out my anxious news to our group, turned, and started to retrace my steps as best I could.

The crowd was so dense that I realised I could walk past him only six feet away, and not see his small three year old form amongst the press of dads, mums, grandparents, and push chairs.

"Oh Lord, please help me find him," I cried out. An overwhelming fear that I might never see him again, and what would happen to my precious son, gripped me fiercely by the throat. My heart pounded.

I walked on, trying to walk in a straight line. If you have ever tried to walk across a field, or parkland, in a straight line on a snowy day, and looked back, you will know how extraordinarily difficult it is to do so.

I felt a nudge to go ever so slightly to the left, so I did. A few dozen more yards and suddenly, there was Andrew, directly in front of me, his face set, stolidly walking forwards. Relief flooded in like a huge cleansing tide and I took his hand in mine.

We walked a bit, and then, concerned, "Are you alright Andrew?"

It was then that the tears came, his, and mine.

Tears of relief, and salvation, and rescue accomplished. Prayers of gratitude and thankfulness pouring out to a loving God who had watched over this little child with such kindness and care. Thankfulness to a God who had given his anxious dad a nudge to bring us both back together in such a precise way. A nudge to show us that it was His hand that guided us both, and that He is, as He promises us, always with us.

Hebrews 13 verse 5. *"Never will I leave you, never will I forsake you."*

Chapter 10
A CAT'S WHISKER ON THE M25
(or, How to create a Parallelogram at 70 mph.)

I have never particularly liked driving along the M25, and I am probably one of a large company of similarly minded people. But, if you want to go from High Wycombe to some place in the London or South East area it is unavoidable. Unless, that is, you are happy to get lost trying to find a way through the confusion of London's streets.

The sun was shining, the traffic wasn't too bad, and the route round the North of London was one of those more pleasant drives for Maria and me as we headed for the M11 and Redbridge.

We were following a black car, which was minding its own business, when a saloon overtook us and eventually caught up with the car ahead of us.

Moments later the car in front of us flipped a complete sideways circle and landed on its tyres. But the shape had changed to what we were told in geometry class was a parallelogram.

To avoid an inevitable collision I stood on the brakes, and came to a dead stop. We were still alive, so far, with just over a car length to spare between us and the car in front.

The car which had overtaken us was facing in the wrong direction, and we were suddenly surrounded by dozens of cars coming to a screeching halt.

It flashed through my mind that it was always the second waive of cars which caused the pile-up. I braced myself for a smash into my boot, asking God for His protection.

I saw a car coming up fast behind me, swerve into a small space to my right, swerve into the space in front of me, and stop dead. As he passed by, I caught a glimpse of relief on the driver's face, as he realised he was going to make it by a cat's whisker.

We did not make it into the News headlines that day because the only cars that were damaged were the two directly involved in the collision.

Everything had gone quiet, and after I had calmed down a bit I looked around. Cars were passing the scene very slowly to my right! Strange!

I deemed it safe to get out of the car. I looked back to see why they were so slow. It was then I saw a line of litter from the collision which could have been purposely laid out. It was a completely straight diagonal, which ended up a few feet to the right of my rear bumper, like so many dark traffic cones guiding the traffic around us.

As I looked at the debris I saw a mobile phone close by. I cannot be sure of course, but was the use of that the cause of the accident? I have often wondered.

I got back into the car and carefully joined the slow moving traffic, my heart still pumping the adrenaline around my system. I thanked God for His answer to my prayer, and for saving so many lives, and preventing so many injuries.

Psalm 121 vv 7-8: *"The Lord will keep you from all harm – He will watch over your life; the Lord will watch over your coming and going both now and forevermore."*

Chapter 11
THE OCCUPATIONAL HAZARD
(or, The really embarrassing one, but I'll tell you anyway.)

I engaged first gear to execute a neat 3-point turn in the pub's tiny yard, which acted as their car park. I pushed down on the accelerator, then the brake, in what I thought was quick succession, and gently bumped the pub's outside wall. This surprised me as I was very good at these manoeuvres, and I hadn't seen it as a challenge.

"Perhaps I've had too much beer to drink after all," I thought.

"Perhaps I ought not to drive," I mused, in a sort of befuddled way.

But then my hotel was too far to walk on unsteady feet, and I needed the car in the morning to get to work.

It was 1972, Derby, and I was one of the receivership/liquidation team for Rolls Royce Ltd., and bored out of my mind.

The Rolls Royce sales team were brilliant and had lined up lots of contracts for the new RB211 engine which was to be made with an exciting new material, carbon fibre. It promised greater strength and durability with a lighter weight. So confident were the sales team that they had agreed delivery dates, and accepted heavy penalties if the engines were not delivered on time.

Looking into the future it was going to be a winner, eventually powering half the world's airliners! Except that in 1971 it wasn't yet out of the experimental stage, and there were a few, as yet, unresolved problems that had cropped up, which often happens with new technology.

The deadline, with its heavy penalties, was approaching faster than the progress in solving the issues. There were also enormous cost overruns which meant that the company was in serious trouble.

It was heading towards bankruptcy, which was really bad news for the town. Rolls Royce was its major employer at that time, and Derby would face mass unemployment. The solution? Receivership, followed by Voluntary Liquidation and the formation of a new company, Rolls Royce (1971) Ltd. Neat, eh? When the company was eventually wound up, all creditors, lenders, and shareholders were repaid in full.

So there I was, helping to prove, or disprove, applications from businesses claiming to be owed money by the company. There are always those who will try to jump on the bandwagon and make false claims. It was important work, but I was getting seriously bored, and learning to get seriously drunk on the generous "entertainment allowance" we were given. It is definitely something I am not proud of, and would warn anyone to avoid like the plague. And, in a way, it is like the plague, because it can kill you off before your time, and totally mess up your life meanwhile.

Now this is not often admitted, but solicitors, barristers, and accountants, have one occupational hazard in common, apart from the tendency of some to be a bit stuffy. In a word, over-drinking.

Alcohol that is, not Pepsi-Max!

So I started on the slippery slope towards alcoholism, which continued over the next twelve years.

It was so gradual that I didn't realise it was happening. Partly maybe, because, a few years down the line, I compared my intake with that of one of my partners. He, I accidentally discovered, and to my astonishment, drank down a 75cl bottle of brandy during the course of the working day. He was so used to it you couldn't tell.

With great pride he boasted that he could drink anyone under the table. However, one Saturday he was found by the office cleaner, collapsed, by his desk, and bleeding to death.

She didn't usually clean on a Saturday morning, but she had other plans for this particular Friday, and so decided to clean on Saturday morning. She arrived just in time to save his life. He died a few years later, hardly reaching early middle age, a proud man, proud of the very accomplishment that eventually destroyed him.

So there I was, at the age of 39, on that same slippery slope, and heading for the same ending, in all probability. Not that I was drinking because I was proud of any achievement with it, but because I rather enjoyed it – too much!

I'm really ashamed of the next bit, but I'll tell you anyway as an example of what to avoid.

The trouble is, I felt critical of people who called themselves Christians, and drank alcohol. I considered myself a Christian, and I drank alcohol – too much of it!

Just a moment! Hold on! What was it Jesus said about being critical of what people do and then doing the same thing yourself? People who criticise others for their failings but make mistakes themselves, even, maybe, the same ones? Who look down on those they think morally inferior? Now what was that term he used?

Oh! That's right!

Hypocrites!

That's trying to make out that we are holier than we really are. That's criticising others for doing wrong things, and not admitting that we do wrong things as well. That's forgetting that we all need to help each other to overcome our temptations, and that we need the help of others, as much as everyone else.

Just as Jesus drew the attention of the Pharisees to their hypocrisy, so, one evening, Jesus drew my attention to my hypocrisy.

I was heartbroken.

"Dear Lord, forgive me for my sin," I cried out, "Have mercy on me. You are right when you say that there is no goodness in me, that I need You in my life or I die. I will never criticise anyone caught in this trap again."

I then remembered what it promises in the Bible, "If you confess your sins, He is faithful and just and will forgive us our sins, and cleanse us from all unrighteousness."

That last part was particularly comforting to me, and I fell asleep that night at peace, knowing that there was a new phase of life ahead.

The next morning I awoke without looking forward to a pint at lunchtime, and without a desire to drink alcohol at all. In fact it was clear to me that God was saying to me that I must never drink alcohol again.

And that is how I came to understand those caught in that same trap of addiction, and my heart goes out to them. Two related incidents are included in this book. See *"The Trouble With Fred"*, and *"Overfilled with Christmas Cheer"*.

I will briefly tell you about two others.

Dave was a small man. He was shorter than me even, which is a reasonable achievement. The trouble was, as a small man, his lifestyle made him so very vulnerable to bullying.

One day he gave his life to Jesus, and it was so good to see him every Sunday raising his hands in praise of his Saviour. It made my heart sing to watch him as he worshipped the One who had made his life meaningful, and who gave him an eternal future in God's Kingdom of Love and Peace. No bullying there.

The thing is that he couldn't kick the alcohol habit.

Don't ask me why God didn't just take him out of it, like He had done for me.

I don't know the answer to that one, but I do know God really loved him, as you will see.

He would come to church smelling like a brewery. I know because I used to look out for him. We often talked, and sometimes sat together. Then he started bringing some of his closest friends, his alcoholic buddies.

He also often brought with him cuts and bruises on his face, and probably elsewhere as well. When I asked him about it he just shrugged. He said that that was the lifestyle of those who led his type of life. That was their scene. Scary!

And then one day he wasn't at church.

A few days later I learnt that he had died the previous Friday night, having choked to death in his sleep, which is not uncommon with alcoholics. The amazing thing was, God arranged not only for him to be found without delay, but to give him a spectacular send-off.

Usually alcoholics don't even get a mention when they die, but God arranged for an obituary usually reserved for royalty, or "really important people" – the front page of the paper no less! Admittedly the local paper, but who else gets mention on the front page of any paper? Not many of us. And certainly not an alcoholic!

The evening he died, three guys decided to break into where he was staying to rob the place – and found his body. It was the sort of bizarre event that newspapers love, and so the story appeared on the front page!

And then there was Carrot, so-called because of his naturally bright red hair which dazzled in the sun.

He begged on the streets, slept rough, and consumed vast amounts of alcohol and drugs. I have seen him literally crawling on all fours to the off-licence (now closed) in Desborough Road, High Wycombe, to buy his three litres of cheap cider.

The manager of the Charity I worked for at the time was really cross with the breweries who made it.

"Brewed specially for the alcoholics," he would say angrily.

It broke my heart.

I was walking down White Hart Street in High Wycombe one day, and Carrot called out, "I can guarantee ... that all donations .... go to a worthwhile cause .... and will be spent on ....booze and drugs," and he gave a huge guffaw.

Christians all over town knew him, talked with him, prayed over him, and loved him. I talked with, and prayed over him myself sometimes, and one day, after a lengthy chat, I asked him if he would like to invite Jesus into his life as He would change his life for the better. I am sure many other Christians had done the same.

"I'm scared to," he said.

When I asked him what the reason for that was, he said that he had suffered a terrible and painful childhood that he was trying to blot out, and didn't know who to trust.

I said that he could trust Jesus, because He loved him, and wanted to give him a better life.

"I can't," he said.

But in fact he did.

Some months later, about Christmas time, the buzz went round town that Carrot had given his life to Jesus, and Christians all over town sang, "Hallelujah"!

A few days later God took him.

I could almost hear God saying to him, "You are now mine, Carrot, and I'm not going to let you suffer any more. Welcome home."

Of course God knew his real name, so I expect He called him home with that, a name which Carrot refused to tell me, and no-one else seemed to know either.

Mind you, God probably gave him a new name, something like "Wonderful Treasure of the Lord God Almighty".

That's just like God.

Isaiah 35 v 10; 51 v11. *"Gladness and joy will overtake them, and sorrow and sighing will flee away. They will enter Zion (God's presence) with singing; and everlasting joy will crown their heads."*

Chapter 12
HOW IT ALL ADDED UP!
(or, An Accountant's Nightmare.)

I found myself laughing out loud as I read the result of my Myers Briggs Personality Profile. It tells you what sort of character you are, and what sort of job is best for you. I had discovered that the job I had trained for, and spent 21 years of my life working in to provide my bread and butter and a bit more, was a job "that will drive you mad"!

The jobs that suited me best were jobs that involved me with people, and gave freedom to be creative.

So that explained a lot!

The boredom, the headaches, and why I loved meeting my small clients; the jobbing builders, farmers, push-bike repairers, and small shopkeepers. I delighted in preparing their accounts, and making sure they only paid the right amount of tax.

I preferred them to the big Building Society audit, the multi-site timber merchants, and the national paper manufacturers, which I also had to audit.

It explained why I spent my time completing a job creatively instead of in a predictably boring accountant's way.

It explained why a friend of Maria and I thought me out of place in an accountants' office.

So, how did I come to be an accountant if it was that bad?

Well, when it was time for me to leave school and find a job, my parents were my job advisory panel. My dad in a negative way, and my mum in a positive way.

Dad was an engineer and steered me away from it calling it 'a mugs game'. That surprised me because he was very good at it, and worked out how to spin reinforced concrete into lampposts, invented a system of reinforcing concrete which is used to this day, and was also Senior Constructional, Civil & Consultant Engineer of Stewarts & Lloyds Ltd., Corby, Northamptonshire, for many years, until he retired. That is why I ended up being born in nearby Kettering – or Ke-rin in the local dialect (which is awful!). I have always thought of engineers as brilliant people, and so needed by our country, and we still do need them. I am always thrilled when I hear young men and women say they want to be an engineer.

The name of the company dad worked for, Stewarts & Lloyds, sort of gives its origins away. It was a Scottish Iron and Steel company which discovered iron ore beneath the meadows and wheat fields of Northamptonshire. So the company came down to dig it up, smelt it into iron, and then convert it into steel, from which they made steel pipes, some of them enormous.

Seeing large areas of countryside being stripped of its topsoil and subsoil, known as 'the overburden', by an enormous machine with tracks like a tank, called a dragline, was a common sight in our part of rural Northamptonshire at the time. The bucket alone was as big as our three bedroomed semi-detached house! One day, my dad took my younger brother and I to see one, and we felt like ants. It seemed that the "cab" was bigger than our Living Room.

In the absence of enough local people who needed jobs, they brought workers from other parts of the country, mainly from Glasgow in Scotland. They built houses for them, and created a sort of distant suburb of that city, like a new Council Estate that had got lost and fetched up in rural Northants.

It called itself 'Corby' after the tiny village it swallowed up, and we locals knew it as a wild place, where there were regular punch-ups and not a nice place to go.

To go back to me deciding what to do for a living, I longed for a job that would take me outside, as I hated school. Not because of the learning, which I mostly loved, but because it wasn't held outside under a tree somewhere, where I could feel the sun on my skin and the rain on my face.

My mum suggested bookkeeping. I replied that I didn't want to be cooped up in a library all my life, I was an outside sort of person. Then she explained that it was about keeping records of money coming in and going out for businesses. As I was good at maths I said, "Ok".

So my dad persuaded an accounting firm in Kettering, which does that sort of thing, to take me on as a trainee. So there I was cooped up in an office all day, instead of a library. I think the library would have been better, as I would have had more excuse to move around the building and meet people.

As an accountant I was always trying to find an excuse to wander away from my desk. That wasn't easy when you had to call out figures from a heavy handwritten Day Book to someone with a heavy handwritten Ledger much of the time.

Ah me, those were the days of large briefcases loaded down with heavy accounting books and papers. Carrying some of them needed quite a bit of strength and energy. You felt that the local gym couldn't keep you fitter.

These days a slimline laptop holds far more information than a whole room full of the enormous handwritten Accounting Books of those days.

So I started my job, and, to begin with, I couldn't understand what it was all about.

Whilst everyone else who joined the firm at the same time as me took to it like so many ducks to water, it took me six months for the penny to drop. However, I didn't give up, and, once I understood what it was all about, there was no stopping me.

I eventually qualified as a Chartered Accountant, and, about ten years later, I became a 'Fellow'. This was a sort of long service award, which came with a bigger annual membership fee to boost the bank account of the Institute of Chartered Accountants in England and Wales. Quite a neat financing move on their part!

On some of my jobs I felt very lonely as I was sometimes given an office to myself. I felt so lonely that I found myself talking and cracking jokes to myself, which weren't always very funny, but it relieved the boredom. And there is something funny about cracking jokes that aren't funny ...... isn't there?

One day I suddenly realised that I had become so used to doing this that I had started to talk to myself when I was with other people. This can be a bit of a dodgy thing to do when so many people are listening in on your private thoughts. You can lose friends that way. Talking to myself? That old adage 'the first signs of madness' springs to mind, so perhaps Messrs. Myers Briggs weren't too far off the mark!

So, after 21 years, and many headaches later, and, latterly, quite a bit of complaining to God about this tediously exhausting job, I came into my office one day, stood by my desk and said,

"God, if this is where You want me to be for the rest of my life then so be it".

A great peace entered my soul and all the discontent vanished. Then words came into my mind.

"Now you are ready for the work I really want you to do."

Within a month my fellow partners ganged up on me and told me that they could no longer work with me; no reason given. A great relief swept through me. Two weeks later they apologised and asked me to stay, but the damage had been done! My trust in them had died, and, more importantly, I had smelt freedom. There was no going back.

So, I moved from a job that never suited me, to a job that really did. An 'out and about' sort of job, with lots of variety. I once counted I wore fifteen different hats, from washer-upper to project manager, entertainer to forward planner, outings organiser to property management. It was a job that dealt with people, looked after people, and allowed me lots of creative time. That job was the setting up and running, in a 'hands on' manner, of an Old Peoples' Home, with my wife, Maria.

My work as an Accountant did mean I could keep our financial records, calculate our tax, and argue successfully with The Inland Revenue (as it was called then) when they got it wrong, which was quite often. I could also work out whether we could afford to increase the number of rooms, and gave me the confidence to lodge Planning Applications.

Over time we built nine single rooms for our residents, our 'family' as Maria preferred to think of us. My job as an accountant also meant that I was used to talking to government officials, and so we got on well with those we had to deal with. Nothing of those hard 21 years was wasted.

So there I sat, reading my Myers Briggs Personality Profile, and laughing my socks off! The best jobs for me were with people and for people, like our Old Peoples' Home.

And the worst jobs?

There, in the third column, just a little way down – 'Accountancy, guaranteed to drive you mad' – or words to that effect.

It all added up!

Proverbs 3 vv 5-6; *"Trust in the Lord with all your heart and do not lean on your own understanding; in all your ways acknowledge Him, and he will make your paths straight."*

Chapter 13
PUTTING MY BACK INTO IT
(or, How I put my back out,
and How I learnt to put it back in again.)

Looking back it was one of those crazy ideas that come to me from time to time. Why I didn't take it round the back of the house and leave it outside, where it really belonged, escapes me. But, there I was, lugging a 25 kilo bag of garden compost up the stairs to store in the (then unused) front bedroom. I suppose I had some logic at the time, but, now, it puzzles me what it was. After three or four steps up I began to sense that "this is not a good idea".

The trouble with my family is that we like to see things through. Mostly that's a strength, but, just now and again, it can backfire.

And so, there I was, lugging this heavy bag of compost up the stairs with my father's "never give up", ringing in my ears. His story of the two frogs in a jug of cream, as an illustration of how persistence pays, resonated in my brain, and that's what I did – didn't give up I mean.

The story of the two frogs? You'd like to hear it?

Well now, two frogs, Croak and Kickit, fell into a jug of fresh, top-of-themilk, cream. Croak gave a few kicks, slithered down the side of the jug, and decided that it was all too slippery, and he would never manage to get to the lip of the jug and jump free. He let himself slither to the bottom of the jug and moped. The little air that there was in the cream was soon used up, and it didn't take long for the cream to block up Croak's lungs, and, sadly, he drowned.

Kickit, however, was made of sterner stuff. He kicked and kicked, telling himself, "I will get out. I will get out." Whilst Croak sank to the bottom, and drowned, Kickit kept on kicking. "I will get out. I will get out," he kept saying to whoever might be listening.

He began to tire, but still he wouldn't give up. He just kept kicking, and repeating, "I will get out. I will get out".

The more he kicked, the thicker the cream got. The thicker the cream got the harder it was to kick. But Kickit just wouldn't stop.

"I will get out. I will get out," he said.

Then, a remarkable thing happened.

"Oh goodness," he thought, "what is this beautiful yellow solid thing it has turned into?" He didn't have a name for it, but then, frogs don't eat butter!

Without further thought, he jumped out of the jug, and went for a cooling swim in his favourite pond.

Back to me and my garden compost. My persistence succeeded in getting the 25 kilo bag to the front bedroom, and I felt really proud of myself. This was immediately followed by an uncomfortable twinge in my back, which quickly developed into serious pain.

What's that old saying about pride?

The pain made it crazy to drive, difficult to concentrate on my work, and disturbed my sleep. I learnt just how much permanent pain wears you down.

About a year later Maria and I were planning to look after elderly infirm people. What eventually became our Old Peoples' Home. This would involve moving and handling those residents who didn't have the strength to do it themselves. Having a bad back means you can't do it.

"Lord," I said, "if this is the job you want me to do I need a strong back, free from pain, don't I? Mine really hurts."

Immediately a thought came into my mind.

I was to go and stand with my back to the back of one of our strong locally made Windsor dining chairs, and then press down really firmly.

So I did.

"Do it again." So I did.

"And once more." So I did.

Result, the pain was gone.

Maybe I could have done this any time during that twelve months, but could it really be a 'lucky thought' or a 'happy coincidence', that the idea of how I was to resolve my back pain followed immediately after my chat with God?

Exodus 15 v 26; *"I am the Lord who heals you."*

Chapter 14
THE WORLD IN A TWIRL
(or, The best time of my life so far)

The unexpected happens so unexpectedly. One minute, there you are, the world going on for you much as usual, and the next minute – well, in my case everything started going round like a carousel trying to beat the land speed record. The world gave a quick twirl, and it wasn't pleasant.

I was just stepping off the bus after a lunch break, and the world decided to show me that it really does spin on its axis, and that it can be really difficult to stand up straight.

I lurched towards a friendly brick wall belonging to an engineering factory and did my best to remain upright, hoping that passers by would not think me drunk – (oh the shame of it!).

I prayed, "O God help me to get back to my place of work," and waited for the whirling world to stop its antics, which were making me feel seriously sick.

The giddiness passed off, and I walked the few yards to where I was doing temporary work without a stagger, much to my thankfulness. As I sat at my desk I soon realised that all was not over yet, and asked a work mate to run me home.

On the way I had to frantically wave to him to stop. I opened the door and was spectacularly sick. As I shut the door my driver took off like a jet fighter pilot on an urgent mission. The indignant stares of passersby chased after us like earth to air missiles.

I arrived home and immediately went and lay on my bed, thinking that this was my last day on earth. The slightest movement set off feelings of incredible sickness. By then we had started our Old People's Home, and I called out to one of our staff and asked her to call an ambulance. She took one look at me and ran for the phone.

At Accident and Emergency a small group of medics hummed, haa'd, and creased their brows about what it might be. After what seemed a long time, one bright spark gave it as his opinion that it was Labarynthitis, an infection of the inner ear.

Relieved at finding a probable diagnosis, they gave me some air sickness tablets and sent me home.

The tablets only took the edge off the giddiness, and I was to lay on my back fighting off nausea for several weeks. I hardly dared to move, which made toileting a bit of an unpleasant and hazardous undertaking.

Friends from church visited me many times, which is one of the many things I like about our church, and their visits really helped to encourage me.

Although ….I felt I was having the best time of my life so far!

Surprised?

I suppose I was at first, but the presence of God was so powerful that I loved it.

I listened to a lot of worship songs; listened to a history of the church through the centuries; and learnt how God had kept the real truth of the Christian faith alive through difficult times, sometimes in just a small number of dedicated disciples.

It was then I learnt to talk to God a lot, and, as importantly, or maybe even more importantly, listen to God a lot.

Because, you see, I believe in a person, not a philosophy or a religion.

In difficult times, as you will know, a philosophy or a religion is not much help. We need a person to be with us. Jesus came to make it possible for us to have a relationship with God, not to have a religion about Him. God promises never to leave us, enjoying the good times with us, and supporting us through the tough times.

So there He was with me, as I struggled with the giddiness and nausea.

When I recovered, I went back to work with renewed vigour; although I did decide not to climb ladders for a bit!

God had been faithful to His promise never to leave me nor forsake me,

Psalm 46 vv 10-11; "Be still and know that I am God; The Lord Almighty is with us."

Chapter 15
THE TROUBLE WITH FRED
(or, The story of A Little Seepage.)

I have a confession to make.

Despite my extensive experience of camping and hiking, cooking over wood fires (you could when I was young), bathing in chilling mountain streams, and clearing up all kinds of unpleasant messes, despite all that, with some things I can be a really fussy kind of a person.

Which makes what happened somewhat amazing.

It wasn't as if it was a special sort of a day. In fact it was quite an ordinary sort of a day. Which only goes to show that miracles can happen just about anytime, and, as events proved, just about anywhere.

It all happened because we wanted to hire a video-tape – you know, one of those old fashioned bulky things with "VHS" printed on the side. You can tell how long ago it was! Not that Fred knew anything about that side of the story, or would have been interested if he had.

However, just as I turned into the road where I usually parked, he attracted my attention from the pavement.

I say, "from the pavement", because he had just stopped himself from falling off it by the simple trick of grabbing hold of a handy pole. The pole's usual job was to support a road sign; but it did its work of supporting Fred quite as well.

I slammed on my brakes and came to an abrupt stop.

Well, I couldn't take my eyes off him, and driving safely when you're not looking where you are going has a trick to it that I don't have.

Fred clung tenaciously to the pole, sinking lower and lower until the embarrassment of sitting in the gutter stared him in the face. Just as all seemed lost, with a supreme effort he jerked himself upward and across the uneven pavement to the stone wall. He slumped against it, momentarily triumphant.

Almost immediately he began to slide to ground level once again.

Not to be beaten, his body convulsed once more and he was off again, his legs jerking this way and that, puppet-like, but somehow propelling him towards the road once more.

This time there was no pole in sight!

My open-mouthed fascination turned to consternation.

Horrors! With nothing to stop him I could see him stagger into the road and get hit by a passing car.

I looked for a pedestrian to call out to, but the pavements were deserted.

Suppressing the panic which fought to rise to the surface, I called out,

"Jesus, please stop him from falling into the road".

I had intended to say, "God, send an angel to hold him", but somehow it came out differently.

I parked as quickly as I could and leapt out. Relief swept over me as I saw Fred clinging for dear life to the arm of an obliging Middle Eastern looking gentleman who seemed to have appeared out of thin air, and who was looking into his befuddled eyes with an amused smile.

It was at that moment that I was sorely tempted to walk away from the whole thing. After all I didn't know him, and someone else was taking care of him, wasn't he? I was free to go. End of story!

Perhaps curiosity got the better of me, or perhaps God had a hand in it, but questions flashed through my mind.

"Is he really drunk? Maybe he's diabetic and needs expert medical help."

I went up to him, and as I stooped over to look into his face to ask, "Are you ok?", the Middle Eastern looking gentleman lifted Fred's hand onto my arm with an "All yours now" sort of gesture.

Fred turned and said something in Chinese, which was strange as he didn't look Chinese. It was accompanied by the unmistakable fragrance of a rugby club beer cellar and my doubts evaporated!

It was at this point that I realised that Fred was insecurely swaying from my arm, and that the Asian looking gentleman had disappeared as completely and quietly as he had appeared.

I looked up the street, down the street, across the road, and then behind me for an alleyway he may have popped into.

Nothing!

Could he have walked the twenty or so feet to the corner in the two seconds it took me to look into Fred's face, say "Are you ok?" and look up again? Lightening could maybe! So what had happened to him? Not only that, I had thought that we were in this together.

What was I to do now?

I experimentally cast Fred adrift upon his tossing sea, and caught him at the edge of the pavement on the next returning wave.

I really couldn't see how he could make it home in one piece on his own. Even if he did, the way he was tacking back and forth across the pavement he was likely to ricochet off everyone within striking distance.

"Where do you live?" I asked, hoping that it wasn't too far. I could see that with Fred a hundred yards was as a mile.

He replied in his quaint Chinese dialect, and indicated impressively down the West Wycombe Road with his left elbow. "Could such a dishevelled person actually have a home?" I wondered.

"How far?" I asked, my hopes fading. The road to West Wycombe is a long one from where I was standing.

Out of the Chinese two words emerged and became distinct, "Chow ming yang tao islly show you".

I became resigned to my new situation and put time to one side.

Taking Fred firmly by the right arm I started walking. After three steps I realised that, if we were to stop looking like a couple of bouncy balls tied together with elastic, I would have to hold him up more securely.

I put my left arm tightly around his shoulders, my right hand under his right arm, took a deep breath, and got under way.

We weren't going to win any prizes for speed, but perhaps recognition for the slowest comedy duo of the year? Can you imagine it?! For some strange reason I felt no embarrassment about it at all. What was going on with me?

We hadn't gone far when I became conscious of an increasingly smelly quality about Fred. It dawned on me that the brewery's Best Bitter had completed its job, and was now clocking off and aiming for the exit.

I began to be aware that certain areas of his clothing were getting damp, and then, as if in sympathy, that mine were getting damp, and then, horrors, I was getting damp. I was no longer too sure what I was hugging.

"Oh well, it will wash," I consoled myself, as more of the warm odour oozed itself through my Persil clean clothes.

I ceased to be bothered about it.

It didn't seem so very long after that we docked at his flat, although later I found we had walked the best part of a mile. I invited myself in to see if his brother was about, and he was happy with that, but his brother was out. He was now speaking in an almost intelligible form of Inebriated Bucks, so we chatted in a left-handed sort of a way for a while; that is, a right-handed sort of a way if you're left handed.

It was then that the first miracle occurred.

He was really cut up about how he lived his life, the things he did, and he wanted out. I talked to him about the Person who loved him more than anyone in the whole wide world. How he could have all those wrong things he so despised about himself forgiven. How that Person would give him the strength and courage to live a better sort of life.

I talked to him about Jesus, and how Jesus wanted to be his friend. He wanted this so much that he welcomed Jesus into his life, to be his Lord for the rest of his life, here and for eternity.

The proof of the pudding is in the eating, the old saying goes. Well, I was up and down the West Wycombe Road in my car several times over the next few weeks.

I often saw him sitting on the wall outside his house happily puffing on a cigarette, and waving cheerily to me as I called out to him. A man dressed and in his right mind.

I reckon that we will see each other again one day, when we both meet Jesus in heaven, and have a good laugh together.

Later that evening, as I sat in my easy chair and dressing gown, listening to the Persil working on my clothes, and letting the excitement of the day ebb away, a revelation began to seep into my conscious mind. Here was yours truly, who hated getting his clothes spotted with water, never mind anything else, calmly reflecting on the events of the afternoon.

It was then that I realised that a second miracle had taken place.

Fussy, pernickety, fastidious, yours truly had been soaked to the skin with an unmentionable wetting agent, and, if I was running true to form, I should be having feelings of discomfort, dirtiness, irreparable tainting, and total insecurity.

To my complete surprise, it dawned on me that I hadn't really minded.

In our erratic walk I had hugged to myself a member of the human race more commonly despised than helped, as the occasional honking of passing cars with a few swear words attached proved.

The remarkable thing was that I came away deeming it a privilege. Will I ever be the same again?

Some people say that they don't believe in miracles.

I think it's because they don't recognise them when they happen. Very often we think we're too intelligent to believe that miracles can happen.

And then, miracles can take many forms. It can be a change in attitude which it is not in our power to make; or it can be a physical event which defies scientific explanation.

In either case there are some who refuse to believe in miracles, despite the evidence. That's because to accept something as a miracle means accepting that there certainly is a God, and that He intervened, and made something happen that is remarkable and out of the ordinary.

Both these miracles were amazing attitude changes.

There was fussy old Alan Edmondson holding up against his clean clothes someone drunk, dirty, and seeping, whom God loves, and I didn't mind.

And then I realised that, actually, in God's eyes, I wasn't all that different from Fred.

"What!" you might say, "You don't get drunk like Fred and join him on the West Wycombe Road playing bumper cars back and forth across the pavement, do you?"

Well, I did have my own problem with alcohol once (see "The Occupational Hazard") but no, I don't do that.

But there are lots of other wrong things I do.

Not heinous crimes like robbing banks or throwing bricks through shop windows, but self-centred things like getting annoyed when I don't get my own way, being greedy, or criticising people.

To God this is no different from robbing a bank or shattering windows, because they are not in His nature to do these things, and He didn't design them to be in mine either.

They all come from the same source. Putting "me" and "what I want" first, instead of thinking of other people's needs as well.

So, I still need as much forgiveness and change as Fred, my new friend.

Psalm 21 verse 4. "He asked you for life and you gave it to him – length of days for ever and ever."

Chapter 16
THE DRAMA OF THE TOPPLING TABLE
(or, How God gave me a hand.)

As my hands closed around the stage prop on the top shelf the table began to collapse sideways under me at an alarmingly rapid rate, threatening to throw me violently onto a row of empty shelves to my left, and only twenty minutes to the opening number of the Musical I was in.

It was the 1980's and a group of us had performed a sketch, or short play, for the church Harvest Festival celebrations, and loved it so much that we had carried on as a Church Drama Company.

We took it seriously enough to teach ourselves theatrical skills from courses we went to, and from reading books. We practiced every week, honing our skills, and began to perform sketches written by Riding Lights, Ambush Theatre, and others, to each of whom we paid a small royalty.

We performed in churches, at celebratory events, at village fetes, and we loved it. We also applied to perform at the annual Town 'Switching on of the Christmas Lights', which, at that time was run by the Local Tradesmen's Guild. We took to the streets in medieval costume, including black tights– surprisingly warm even during those cold Autumns – and we were surprised at how quickly a crowd gathered.

There's always something rather appealing about Open Air Theatre.

During that time we also performed two short musicals. One written by an Australian, and the other home grown, including the music.

And we loved it even more!

The Australian Musical was, 'The King is Coming Back', recommended by one of our actors who had performed it over on the other side of the world, right there in Australia.

It involved most of the cast dressing up as clowns, and two of them, during a break in the dress rehearsal, decided that they were hungry. So, in full clown makeup and costume, they went down to the local McDonalds. They must have caused quite a stir!

A band was set up, and actor and band rehearsals ran side by side, then ran together, and then … the Big Day!

The opening number of the Musical was only twenty minutes away, and, thank goodness, there it was! The stage prop I had been searching for was on the top shelf.

Being a short sort of person, my 5 foot 5 inches just wasn't enough to reach it.

Oh no!

There was no time to fetch a ladder, and in front of me was a stout looking table anyway. I gave it an experimental push and pull, and as all seemed well I hopped up onto it and reached for the stage prop.

As my hands closed around it the table began to collapse sideways. There I was, helpless, being flung with ever increasing speed towards the aforesaid rows of empty shelves, which promised me violent pain and bruising, and possibly me out of the show, and maybe having to cancel the performance at the last moment.

"Lord, they need me," I cried out, 'they' being the rest of the Cast, my fellow actors. I closed with the shelves, and, totally off balance, braced myself for the pain of sharp edges and corners cutting into my body and head, and fell onto ….. something firm and protective like the palm of an enormous hand.

I began to collapse into what would be a crumpled heap on the floor with possible damage to bones and muscles, …… but felt myself being straightened up, and positioned firmly on both feet in perfect balance.

I stood there for a moment, slightly dazed, re-running the whole sequence of events, wondering if I had dreamed it all.

But there was the collapsed table, the prop safely in my hand, and me, though dazed, undamaged.

Then, with a "Thank you, thank you Lord, thank you", I rushed off to deliver the prop in time for the opening number, and to play my part in the Musical.

Deuteronomy 33 verse 27: *"The Eternal God is your refuge, and underneath are the Everlasting Arms."*

Chapter 17
GETTING STRANGLED BY A WASP
(or, How I nearly didn't get to write this book Part 4.)

Sometimes, possibly more often than I like to admit to myself, I do something really foolhardy, thoughtless, or crazy, and sometimes all three at the same time. This incident in my life was all three at the same time.

I lost my fear of wasps in early childhood, having met several and disposed of them pretty neatly and without pain to myself. So, I had possibly became a little overconfident in my ability to deal with them when the occasion arose.

One hot sunny day in August, my eldest son Andrew and I were dismantling a shed. On the floor where we were working dozens of overripe wild plums were exciting a similar number of wasps, which had got tipsy on the sweet juices.

Having no fear of, and no respect for, wasps, I was happy to ignore the little creatures buzzing around my ankles, until one of them had the nerve to crawl inside my shirt. I decided, in an inattentive and vaguely thoughtless sort of way, to crush it against my chest to kill it.

Except that the result caught my attention pretty fast.

The wasp's annoyed reaction was predictable and immediate. Sting, sting, sting!

Thinking to kill the blighter that had the nerve to puncture me in this way, I pressed it all the harder – the really thoughtless bit – squeezing more venom into my system.

Feeling it still crawling around I opened my shirt and shoo'd it off, (that was a better idea), and carried on with what I was doing.

Until, that is, I noticed raised patches appearing on my arms, ("hives" in medical terms), and a growing sense of impending departure from this world of overripe plums, woozy wasps, and partly dismantled sheds.

"It's got me!" I said to Andrew my son.

"What?" he asked, looking puzzled.

"A wasp! It stung me and I'm having an anaphylactic fit."

"Anaphylactic fit?"

"An allergic response of my body, which could kill me quite quickly."

I found Maria and told her the sobering news, but first we ran Andrew home. Then, sensing the sweaty smell that is the common result of a man working hard on a hot sunny day, she suggested I have a shower first.

"You can't go to A&E smelling of sweat, can you!"

Can't you?

"I don't think we have time," I said, the sense of impending doom gaining ground by the second.

So we skipped that, and drove unhurriedly down to the hospital, with me saying things like how I had appreciated her agreeing to be my wife, and what a good a wife she was, and to bury me or cremate me according to what the family wanted, as I would be past caring.

As we drove down Bowerdean Road I began to feel better as the adrenaline kicked in, and almost told Maria that I was alright now. After a few minutes it became clear that I wasn't, and that my contract with Planet Earth was definitely terminating.

At A & E they pumped me full of adrenaline and antihistamine, which ruined my heart for ever but saved my life.

For those asking, "Tell me more about an anaphylactic fit", it's an over-reaction of the body which causes swelling, and, importantly, swelling in the throat, which eventually cuts off the air supply and, basically, strangles you to death.

Not a happy way to go.

I was told I had to carry an adrenaline shot in a syringe with me wherever I went, which I did for many years. I even made a special little denim pouch to carry it in, which I fixed to my belt. Real swanky.

However, despite medical opinion insisting that once you need it you need it for the rest of your life, I no longer carry one with me, because I found out that I no longer need it.

So how did I find that out?

Well, the church I belonged to at that time prays for people to be healed, as many churches do. God is kind and gracious, and He has healed many people over the weeks and years, just like you read about in The Bible.

At one midweek meeting the elder leading the meeting asked for those who had a particular physical problem, (I forget what), to raise their hands. Only a few of us did, which is why I ended up surrounded by dozens of people eager to pray for me.

As this huge group started to pray for my healing my skin suddenly felt red hot.

I had a picture of myself with my skin on fire, and the tissue beneath it glowing brightly.

Words came into my head, "I have healed you from anaphylaxis".

What I had put my hand up for I have no idea. God clearly chooses how He will respond to our prayers, and what He will heal. And ...... how He will prove you've been healed.

A short while later I was tidying up at the back of our garden. I was trying to tug free a small tree branch from a heap of tangled garden waste, when I suddenly became conscious of an angry buzzing.

Out of the tangled heap flew three wasps in perfect fighter flight formation, stitched three stings across my chest, (another hot day), and, still in perfect formation, returned to base, job done.

I made a tactical withdrawal, swallowed an antihistamine, and thought about an adrenaline shot.

But, "I have healed you from anaphylaxis", rang in my head.

So I thought I would wait a little, and if the hives re-appeared I would then give myself a shot.

So I waited ... and waited ... and waited ... and ... nothing happened.

I was indeed healed!

I thanked God for healing me, and for the three stings of three wasps, uncomfortable as they were, that He had sent to prove it to me.

Mark 16 vv 17-18;(Jesus said to them), "And these signs will accompany those who believe: in My Name they will drive out demons; they will pick up snakes with their hands; and when they drink deadly poison it will not hurt them at all; they will place their hands on sick people and they will get well."

Chapter 18
THE BIG BANG
(or, How I nearly bought it at an Estate Agents)

I suppose we all have little things that we like doing which seem somewhat bizarre to others.

One thing which Maria has learnt to be patient with, is me looking in Estate Agents' windows to see what's for sale and for how much. Don't ask me why I do it, I just do; like some people enjoy playing golf, tiddlywinks, or licking ice lollies.

Whenever I went into High Wycombe town centre on a quick errand, I would park my car in one of the 15 minute bays in Easton Street. In those days it was one way, and there was room on the right to have a few parking bays. I always looked to see if there was a free one, and, if one was available, it was there I parked.

On my way to the High Street, having parked my car, there was one Estate Agent's window I always spent a few minutes looking into. It was a harmless habit of mine.

Then came the day of the Big Bang.

I was on another quick errand. As I turned into Easton Street I decided that today I would park in the nearby multi-storey car park, even though there were several 15 minute bays empty, and my errand wouldn't take very long.

I was in one of my (many) "Let's have a change today" moods, which is another thing Maria has learnt to accept, to humour me.

I found myself ascending floor after floor without finding a parking space, but not really minding.

I arrived on the top floor and parked. As I came down the steps I heard an almighty bang. I looked over the side of the car park and listened, but could hear nothing more.

79

Puzzled as to what it could have been, I continued on down the stairs, dismissing it as one of those odd things that just happen.

As I emerged onto the street I stopped, my brain trying to make sense of what I saw.

A lorry had partly buried itself into the office of the Estate Agents I usually stopped at, dust still curling up from the gaps between the lorry and the inside walls of the offices.

Several people were standing around, too shocked to talk. It took me a few minutes for my brain to accept what I was looking at. It looked serious.

And serious it was.

The local paper reported that the lorry's brakes had failed on the steep Crendon Street. The momentum of the heavy vehicle made it impossible for the driver to turn it into Easton Street and away from the shops and offices.

An Estate Agent adviser and her client had died instantly, and the manager escaped death by inches as he leaned over to answer his desk phone at just the critical moment.

The lorry driver was in serious shock, and took several weeks to recover.

I have often wondered. Was it God who influenced me to pay and park that one time when I really shouldn't be looking at the houses for sale?

Isaiah 48 verse 17: *"I am the Lord your God, who directs you in the way you should go."*

Chapter 19
THE INCIDENT AT WOUNDED KNEE
(or, The Floor Show to end All Floor Shows.)

As a Social Sportsman the possibility of a sports injury never occurred to me. Surely that only happened to professionals and Olympic and Club level players, right?

Wrong!

At the age of fifty something there I was with one!

Wha-a-a-at!

"How did that happen?" you might ask.

Apart from trotting round our local park and neighbourhood on my own, which was quite boring, I played myself at squash for a few months to sharpen my reaction times, for what, I haven't the faintest idea, and every week, for some years, Maria and I played badminton with friends of ours at the local Sports Centre.

These matches were always really comical, mostly because we were there to enjoy ourselves and never stopped disrupting the serious players with our hysterical laughter.

But also because Maria is five foot and a halfpence tall, and slender, and I am just five inches taller and slightly plump, and our friends are five foot ten and six foot three, broad and plump. Our plumpness was partly why three of us were playing!

We mostly played as one couple against the other couple, The Midgets against The Giants!

But the last set of games, the best of three, was always The Husbands against The Wives. This meant that only two games were ever played because The Wives were always changing the rules, and The Husbands were Gentlemen, and never objected!

We always said that anyone hoping to pick up the game of Badminton from us would surely end up either totally confused, or put off by the complexity of the rules!

The thing about squash and badminton is all those sudden stops, mostly on the 'leading leg'. Eventually the knee ligaments on my leading leg, the right one, began to object and started to leave their anchorage points for pastures new.

This meant I found it excruciating to walk upstairs, and, before taking the first step upwards, I learnt to pause, grab my right knee, grimace, and say "ouch" (goodness knows why that helped) like one of the characters in Lewis Carroll's famous book 'Alice Through the Looking Glass'.

Then came that Sunday.

In those days our church used to invite people to the front to be prayed for every Sunday, and we were not a shy lot. Lots of people would walk forward for prayer, and I was a prayer team fella who prayed for people.

This particular morning I hung back, but so many people were waiting to be prayed for I thought I had better go and join the team.

As I came round the back of a very tall person, our senior elder emerged, coming the other way with a small bottle of olive oil in his hand, and asked me if I had come out for prayer.

"Oh!" I said, "I came out to pray for someone, but yes, please, I'm having trouble with my right knee."

Obeying the instructions in James 5 v 14 (see below), he dipped his finger in the olive oil, made the sign of the cross on my forehead with it, which was quite cooling and greasy, and then ....

POW!!

A great bolt of energy hit me and knocked the breath out of me.

I collapsed into someone's waiting arms, who gently lowered me to the ground.

This often happened when people were prayed for, so we used to pray in two's. One person stood behind the one who was being prayed for as a "Catcher", so they wouldn't get hurt when they collapsed.

The same someone, I was too dazed to notice who, straightened my legs, and then bent the right foot so that it was vertical. He then pushed the sole of my foot firmly upright, as if preparing it for what was to follow then he gave it a final push as if to make sure it was in the correct position.

"How did he know to do that?" I wondered.

It wasn't until some days later that I thought, "How did I know he was to do that, so I could ask myself, 'How did he know to do that?'", if you follow me.

I lay there a long time, conscious of something going on within and around my knee joint, and knowing I shouldn't interrupt.

After a while my dazed mind began to return to a semblance of normality, and I noticed that the room was emptying. No-one was in the least bit bothered about me lying there taking my time.

At two or three points it seemed the manipulation in my knee had finished so I tried to get up. But I only got as far as lifting my chin. It was like someone was holding me down until the job was done.

More time passed, quite pleasantly, and eventually I sensed I could get up, so I got to my feet.

Our senior pastor looked at me with a slightly amused, quizzical, but friendly look on his face, but I was too dazed to say anything.

I decided to go for a coffee and try to get my wits back together. So I started to walk ....except ...... no, it wasn't a walk, rather some tottery shambolic steps, aimed in the general direction of the coffee pot.

Because of the pain in my knee I had subconsciously learnt a funny walk to lessen the pain. Now the pain was gone I had to learn to walk normally again.

So there I was, tottering my way to a coffee cup, and feeling thankful, pleased and dazed. Our senior pastor joked that I was the only person he knew whose knee had been healed but who couldn't walk afterwards!

It seems it was a good repair job rather than a total reconstruction, and once in a purple moon it can feel uncomfortable. All that I need to do is put on a knee bandage, and after a couple of days it is as right as rain again.

Since then I have walked miles, climbed hills, ascended stairs, and Larnaca's nine inch kerbs, without pain or discomfort, or any thought about my right knee.

I thank God for His Love for me in taking the trouble to heal my wounded knee.

James letter: Chapter 5 verses 14 & 15. "Is any one of you sick? He should call the elders of the church to pray over him and anoint him with oil in the name of the Lord, and the prayer offered in faith will make the sick person well; the Lord will raise him up."

P.S. If you are wondering where Larnaca is, it is a sea port, and the main International Airport, on the south coast of Cyprus. They land some wonderful fish there, which you can buy at The Fishermen's Harbour in McKenzie District.

Chapter 20
THE DISAPPEARING STATUE
(or, How I got Swept off my Feet.)

"You need to stop work immediately and rest up for at least three months. Go away on holiday for three or four weeks. You need complete rest."

I was visiting a Charity which had people working overseas on stressful jobs. On their return to the United Kingdom it was their habit to give their workers a stress test.

I was delivering something, and the person I had gone to meet took one look at me and asked me to fill in their stress questionnaire.

I scored 9 out of 10!

"Stop work immediately." he said.

I thought, "I can't."

The thing was Maria and I were looking after Elderly Infirm people and it was a job you can't just stop doing.

Maria looked after the care side and the care staff, and I did most other things from Business Planner to Plumber, from Project Manager to Supplies Purchaser, from Accounts and Payroll to Painter and Decorator, from Chatterbox to Arguer with the Inspection Team, who visited us twice a year to make sure we were keeping to the rules, which we always were.

We were full, but we didn't earn enough to pay someone else to do my job.

What to do?

This was in 1994, and we started talking about selling the Old People's Home we had set up and loved. This was particularly difficult for Maria, who had dreamt of owning such a place, and who was blessing the socks off our Elderly Residents, as well as those who were part of the Carers Team who were caring for them.

What to do indeed!

Twice I had to go away on a fortnight's break on my own, to refresh myself, and eventually we agreed to sell the Home.

It was then that we found that, although setting up the Home needed a lot of determination and resilience, selling it was a totally different ball game, and needed a whole lot more determination and resilience.

We eventually found a couple who wanted to take over from us. We agreed terms and they became partners. I sighed a sigh of relief and waited to take a back seat.

But there was a snag.

They needed training to be accepted by the Registration Authority. It was down to us to train them, and this took three years.

During that time life became even more hectic, instead of less. On top of that I took on other responsibilities which, if I had not been so exhausted, I would have had the wisdom not to take on.

And then, 2004 arrived.

I woke up one morning, just a few days before our new partners were to take over completely, and I found that I couldn't remember the events of the last two years.

Except for a vision.

Sometime during those two years I had seen myself standing in a sandy desert. The wind rose, lifting the sand, and creating a sandstorm, which began to blow over me.

At first all was fine, but, as the wind drove the sand over me, my head and a shoulder began to wear away.

It continued to blow hard, and all my head and both shoulders were worn away. My chest, and then my stomach, quickly followed.

To my horror my legs began to disappear. The windblown sand continued to wear them away, until only my ankles and my feet were left.

I watched, horrified, as my ankles began to disappear, quickly followed by my feet, until all that was left were the imprints of my two feet in the sand.

"At least there are the imprints of my feet to show that I once existed," I thought.

And then the wind blew the sand gently into the imprints until they too had gone.

Nothing left to show that I had ever existed.

Words filled my head.

"But I can rebuild you Alan."

I knew it was God speaking to me.

The impression was that He would rebuild me into someone better. A sort of death of the old self, and a birth of a new self. I thanked Him for His Mercy and His presence with me, so faithful to me.

It had taken ten years from being told I must stop all work immediately, until the time when I was able to do so. All that time I was coping with the strength God was giving me, as I prayed pretty well daily to refresh and empower me for what I had to do that day. God and I drew very close during this time, and that sense of closeness is with me to this day.

I am very conscious of God's presence with me, and if a doubt starts to cloud my mind, which is rare, I declare the Truth that He will never leave me nor forsake me.

I have found that God is faithful to all His promises, and my life events have proved it beyond any doubt.

Some time later a neighbour asked, "Do you still have an interest in Keep Hill Rest Home?"

The question puzzled me.

"No. Not for twelve years or more now." I replied. "Why?"

"I Googled your name and you are listed as being a partner in Keep Hill Rest Home, a Limited Liability Partnership."

"What?" I thought, "What Limited Liability Partnership? I don't remember a Limited Liability Partnership."

When I was alone, I looked up my name on the internet, and, sure enough, there I was, listed as a former partner of "Keep Hill Rest Home LLP".

And it was me who had registered it!

I still couldn't remember doing it. I couldn't remember anything about it.

Gradually some events have slotted back into place, although they do still have the feeling of being "those empty years".

It's not something I feel I need to bother about though. I am just thankful that God stayed with me during those totally exhausting years, and enabled me to do things that I most certainly couldn't have done without Him.

Psalm 116 vv 8-9 & 7: "For you, O Lord, have delivered my soul from death, my eyes from tears, my feet from stumbling, that I may walk before the Lord in the land of the living. Be at rest once more, O my soul, for the Lord has been good to you."

Chapter 21
OVERFILLED WITH CHRISTMAS CHEER
(or, The Case of the Legless Roofer.)

At my previous church in High Wycombe, we had, for many years, an increasingly popular and spectacular Christmas Carol Service, which, at the last count, ran four times over their two sites to over 1500 people.

I had the privilege of playing a small part in these services. A drama sketch one year, a dramatised reading another, a solo, very often singing in the choir, where I rumbled around in 1st or 2nd bass as required by the Musical Director.

Singing, particularly Christian songs, always lifts me high. This particular year, after three Carol Services, I was feeling particularly hyper, floating around on cloud nine you might say.

As I set out for home I was walking in a crazily euphoric state of mind, feeling drunk with the beauty of the carols and the choir's 'special piece'.

I wandered aimlessly in the general direction of home, not caring very much how I got there. On I went through the winding maze and echoing corridors of the empty, late night, Eden Centre. Out into the High Street, past the traffic lights into Easton Street, and eventually emerged onto the London Road.

For some strange reason I stayed on the North side of the road. Strange because to get to my home I should have crossed to the South side, as usual, the side where The Rye Park and Keep Hill is, but I just didn't care.

Traffic was almost non-existent, and I wasn't hurrying.

I suddenly noticed that I was catching up with a gentleman of about my size (that is, fairly short) who was weaving his way down the pavement ahead of me.

He decided to weave his way across the road, but lost himself en route and ended up on the same side he started from.

He tried this twice more and lost himself twice more, which must have been quite perplexing.

By this time I had caught up with him.

As he seemed to need help in keeping a straight line, and so achieve his desire to cross the road, I caught hold of his arm.

"You must have had really good evening," I said, with that sense of camaraderie that occurs when two fellas who are feeling really happy meet up, even though for different reasons.

He accepted my help as if I was his brother, and had known me all my life.

We walked on together, on the correct side of the road for us both.

"Have you far to go?" I asked.

He replied in Colloquial British Booze that he lived just a little way down the road.

"Oh, I'm going that way myself," I said, having just decided that that is what I would do. "I'll give you a hand if you like," to which he said that he would be pleased if I did.

He looked at me, weighing me up, and came to a startling conclusion.

"You must be an angel," he said.

There's no accounting for what people see when they are in a confused state of mind. I do believe in angels, they live in my experience as other events in this book record, but I am not one of them.

"Oh no. No!" I replied, "I'm not an angel. Just another human being."

He looked at me with disbelief.

Wanting to get off the subject I asked, "What job do you do? I suppose you're off tomorrow?"

It was easy to see that the quantity of alcohol flooding through his veins would keep him going tomorrow as well, without any more demand on the money in his wallet. Assuming, that is, that he had any left.

"No," he said, "I have to go to work tomorrow. I'm a roofer."

A picture of this legless roofer trying to keep his inebriated balance on a sloping roof flashed into my mind and filled me with fear for the safety of my new friend.

"A roofer!" I exclaimed. "That's a bit of a balancing act. I think you'd better stay at home tomorrow. You're still a bit too happy for climbing over roofs, and I think your happiness will last well into tomorrow."

I was still helping him keep on track, and stopping him tacking back across the road to the North side, or alternatively into the hedge. He didn't seem to mind which.

He looked at me again, quizzically, and made up his mind.

"I think you're my guardian angel," he said with finality, as he turned into a driveway.

"No, no," I insisted. "Just an ordinary sort of a bloke. Not an angel."

He looked at me again, clearly not believing me.

We came to the point where we had all but reached the front door. He'd fumbled his key out, and we were sandwiched between a large van, the wall of the house, and, in front of us, a hedge. I decided he couldn't go far wrong now, and I could leave.

"Just don't go to work tomorrow, will you," I said. "I really don't think you would be safe. You're, well, sort of overfilled with Christmas Cheer, which isn't terribly helpful if you want to keep your balance on a roof."

He looked at me wide-eyed, which is quite easy when you are in his condition.

"I hope you have a good night's sleep," I said as I put a friendly hand on his shoulder. "I'm so glad I met you."

I had developed a really warm feeling towards him, and genuinely didn't want him to crash out of life the next morning.

Then, as I turned to go ....

"I think you're my guardian angel."

The thing about people who have had just a bit too much Christmas Cheer is that once they get an idea into their head it takes an awful lot of shifting. So I didn't contradict him, but smiled, gave him a cheerful waive and headed home.

And this is how a man drunk in God's Holy Spirit met a man drunk on alcoholic spirits, and they became friends, and parted with goodwill on both sides.

I remember praying to God for him on my way home, that God would make sure that my new friend didn't go to work the next day, and that He would draw him close to Himself.

Idling along, and thinking about all that had happened, I became convinced that God had engineered the whole thing.

I thought, "Why did I wander aimlessly about when normally I would head straight home with a big grin on my face to puzzle the local population?"

My own belief is that God caused me to lose time so that I would meet my new friend at just the right moment, so that I could help him safely home, and he would tell me he was a roofer, and I could advise him to skip work the next day, and he would think I was his Guardian Angel, and so take a bit of notice of what I said.

It was God looking after him through me, His servant.

God's like that.

And maybe it is a bit like being a guardian angel after all.

Interesting thought!

But no, you're right, I'm not one. I'm just another very ordinary human being.

Isaiah 40 v 11: "He gathers the lambs in His arms and carries them close to His heart."

Chapter 22
DEATH IS NO STRANGER
(or, How staying motionless saved my life.)

As I walked down Desborough Road in High Wycombe to my doctor's appointment I suddenly thought, "There is something wrong down there," meaning the area around my lower abdomen. It was August 2016.

For the first time it felt really uncomfortable. And that is the strange thing about my condition; you don't know you've got it until it's too late. Unless, that is, you have been having the recommended test; which most men, and some doctors, can't be bothered with.

I sat down in my doctor's surgery and opened with, "I have been experiencing a drop off in energy levels over the last few years, which I thought was just the ageing process. I did notice that I was losing it a little faster than others of my age, but thought that was just me. However, over the last three to four months I have had a rapid loss of energy, which seems to indicate that something, somewhere, is wrong."

As he listened, my doctor was pulling up my notes on his computer screen. He scrolled down, paused, and stiffened slightly.

Searching my face he said, "You had a blood test two years ago that showed a PSA reading of 46. Did you follow that up?"

I didn't realise then the full import of what he was saying.

I had heard about PSA tests, and thought I probably needed to arrange one sometime, but never got around to it.

"I didn't know I had been tested for that," I replied. "Certainly no-one told me about it. I did phone up for the results of my blood test and was told that everything was fine."

"I will arrange for an immediate blood test," he replied, "and an appointment with the oncologist."

Oncologist? Who or what is an oncologist? My ignorance was profound.

And so the NHS sprang into action.

My PSA was 96, and my Gleeson Score, which tells you the severity of the condition, was 9 out of 10. Thankfully the cancer had not spread through the lymphatic system to other parts of my body, or I would have scored 10 out of 10!

This was learnt after several quite uncomfortable tests, like snipping fourteen bits off my prostate!

Yes, indeed, I had that particularly male version of cancer, cancer of the prostate. I didn't realise just how seriously advanced it was until much later, when I learnt that they like to start tests when the PSA result is higher than six!

I was quickly booked in to have 37 radiotherapy treatments at the Churchill Hospital in Oxford, part of the Oxford University NHS Trust. So I can now say that I attended Oxford University! This was always an unreachable ambition of mine at school, but persistence pays, even though I had to use the subterfuge of prostate cancer, and was there for only 7 weeks and 2 days!

I think my wife, Maria, was more concerned than I about the cancer. I was just pleased that they had worked out what was wrong with me. I had come to terms with the possibility of death several times in my life.

The *possibility* of death? What am I saying! Isn't death inevitable, something that happens to all of us?

However, what I had glimpsed when I was 21 (see "Steps to Heaven") lay ahead of me. I would live with Jesus for ever, not because I am a good person, but because I had accepted God's way for the forgiveness of my sins, and accepted His work in my life to live a better way whilst I am on this earth.

When I leave this broken world, as we all must one day, whether we like it or not, I know with certainty that I will live in His Presence, in His Kingdom of Eternal Life and Love, for ever. God promises it, and I believe He keeps His promises – always.

The question is, "Where will your spirit be for ever? Will it be with God, (that is, Father, Jesus, and Holy Spirit) in Joy and Peace; or Hell, floating in darkness and deep despair?" (See "The Watery Grave")

The eternal question with eternal consequences is, "Which will you choose?"

The question is the same for each one of us.

To return to my cancer treatment; I found the preparation for the radiotherapy hilarious despite it being incredibly uncomfortable. You may think me mad for saying so, but I did. Well, you have to keep your sense of humour at such times, even if you are the butt of the joke.

First, I had three pellets of gold, each about the size of a small piece of rice, injected into my prostate. This gave me the most valuable prostate in my family – in money terms that is, otherwise it's the one you don't really want to have.

The person inserting them used an enormous quantity of iodine around the site, and it hurt more than the snips off my prostate taken earlier! This really disappointed the nurse, as she had reassured me that it would be far less uncomfortable. Ah well, such is life, and it was serving a useful purpose, so no problem.

It was followed by three little tattooed spots of about the same size, one on each hip and another on the lower abdomen. These were carefully lined up with the gold pellets so that the rays from the radiotherapy machine would hit the cancer cells accurately – no mistakes!

I've never wanted a tattoo; I can't see the point of them, particularly as they are so expensive. I now have three of them, for life, paid for by the NHS, not that you'd notice, and I'm definitely not showing them off to anyone!

Then the day of my first radiotherapy session dawns.

On arrival I check if my radiotherapy machine, one of five "Varians", is running on time. If not, I note the time it is likely to be ready for me.

I then calculate the time when I have to take the first two cups of water, which have to be drunk one hour before my scheduled time. I must gulp them straight down.

Half an hour before the Varian is ready for me, I have to gulp a further four cups straight down. This creates a volume of just over one litre of water making its way down through my digestive system to my bladder, and gives me the habit of gulping water straight down for the rest of my life.

The idea is that my bladder swells so that most of it moves out of harms way; away from the Varian's penetrating rays. Kill the cancer not your bladder. Good idea!

The problem comes when there is a sudden delay. I then find that holding in one litre of water is quite excruciating after a time, and I have to go and get permission to let some of it out.

I then have to drink another cup!

I become good at waste-water management, and this includes the essential skill, after a session has finished, of running down the corridor holding my trousers up with one hand, not bothering with my belt or zip. Fortunately I never get to the desperation of one man who carried his trousers over his arm as he dashed down the corridor in his underpants in search of an elusive unoccupied loo.

Then there's the self-administered enema. This is designed to remove from the scene anything that would obstruct the Varian's rays. Suffice to say it is another skill one has to learn, and hope will never have to use again.

Then comes the treatment itself. I climb up onto a metal bed. My head and my feet rest in special moulds made for the purpose, and a chock is put under my knees. These are designed to help me stay motionless.

THE LITTLE BOOK OF BIG MIRACLES

Then the experts carefully position the treatment site.

They move my lower body this way, and … no … too much … oh dear, not enough … and a tiny bit more, and … oh-oh-oh … better start again!

Finally they are satisfied and tell me to keep absolutely still. This is made easier by the moulds holding my head and feet motionless, and the chock under my knees.

I decide to think of myself as a dead weight trying to force my way through the metal bed – I know, another crazy idea – but it works, and I don't find it difficult to stay motionless.

Above me a huge round machine on an arm starts buzzing and bleeping and moving purposefully around me; above me, below me, to the side of me, and me trying not to take any notice.

I start thanking God for my treatment, for the nurses and their kindness, for the technicians who keep it all going, and before long burst into praise songs to God.

Well no, the treatment room doesn't vibrate with my singing. It has to be all in my head. I have been warned not to talk, never mind sing my head off.

"It puts the body out of alignment, and we would have to stop and come and adjust you all over again."

Oh no, not all that again.

The evening before my first visit to The Churchill Hospital, I ask God if this is my homecall, or if He wants me on this earth for a little longer for some purpose.

Later that evening I am reading the Bible passage for that day's devotional, and, as I often do, read on.

I am reading Isaiah, and come across Chapter 41. As I come to verse 16, an impression comes into my head,

"Read that again."

I shake my head, not quite sure what I had heard, but backtrack a bit and my eyes alight on verse 8.

I start reading from there, and you can read it all for yourself, but I will summarise it. This is essentially what God says to me.

"You are my servant and I love you. So do not fear, for I am with you. I will strengthen you and help you. Those who oppose you will be as nothing and perish. Though you search for your enemies you will not find them. Do not be afraid, for I myself will help you."

I give credit to the technology that enabled me to receive effective treatment. I am thankful to the doctors, consultants, and specialist nurses, who were so kind, understanding, and helpful to me. I am grateful to all those friends who willingly gave their time to run me over to Oxford, and then waited patiently whilst I prepared for, and received, treatment.

Especial thanks to those who were there when a Varian broke down, which happened several times, and which often meant a long wait for another to become available. Thanks especially to Maria, who not only took me twice a week, but was patient with the weakness and the craziness that the cancer, the radiotherapy, and the post-treatment "treatment" caused.

The day after my last radiotherapy session I was exhilarated! I was so happy.

No more travelling to Oxford, drinking a litre or so of water and coping with water management. No more self-administered micro enemas. No more lying motionless on a metal bed and rushing for the toilet afterwards.

However, the next day, Sunday, it really hit me. What a nightmare it had all been. I had to go for a very long walk to settle down and begin my return to feelings of normality; which took a very long time.

Despite the skilful treatment they were planning to give me, I got the impression that the medical profession were not convinced I would get out of this alive. When it was all over and my PSA read 0.32, I can only say that God was faithful to His promise and it was He who made sure that the cancer was completely destroyed.

My post-treatment "treatment" is another story, one that I will probably never tell. The idea is to prevent the cancer from rearing its ugly head ever again, and I found it most unpleasant, more unpleasant than the radiotherapy. But at least I am alive today to tell you my story.

My last radio therapy treatment was in January 2017. My last PSA reading before writing this, taken on the 3rd October 2023, was 0.34, a far cry from the reading of 96 in August 2016.

Psalm 18 vv 4, 6, 16, 17.

"The cords of death entangled me, the torrents of death confronted me. In my distress I called to the Lord, I cried to my God for help. He reached down from on high and took hold of me; he drew me out of deep waters. He rescued me from my powerful enemy, from my foes, who were too strong for me."

Chapter 23
THE ANGEL ON THE A40
(or, How going to the loo was nearly the last thing I did.)

Just in case you are dipping in and out of this book, I am repeating some of what I have included in the previous chapter so that what I am about to tell you makes sense. I have purposely said it in a slightly different way, so that those who have read the previous chapter don't get bored! So ... onward ...!

Maybe I've got a bizarre sense of humour, but the preparation for my prostate cancer treatment struck me as hysterically funny. Sometimes so much so that I chuckled out loud, which caused a few heads to turn in concern and puzzlement. Who can laugh at a time like this? Well, see what you think.

It went like this.

You turn up at The Churchill Hospital, Oxford, at least one hour before your treatment and check how your radiotherapy machine is doing. That is, whether it is on time, how many minutes late, or not working at all.

From that you work out when it will be ready for you.

One hour before that time you drink two 200 ml. cups of water straight down. Thirty minutes later you check to see when your machine will be ready, and half an hour before that time drink four 200 ml. cups straight down.

You've got it! Your bladder is getting rather full!

The idea is that your bladder is extended, and mostly out of the way of the strong radio waves they use to kill the cancer. And this does two things. Firstly, it limits the damage which it would otherwise do to your bladder, and secondly, the gamma waves have better access to the treatment area.

So far so good.

You also have to give yourself a micro enema, but the less said about that the better, although it is part of the hysterically funny story. This also shifts stuff out of the way of the gamma rays.

If everything is on time then it works well, and you can control the inevitable feeling of wanting to rush to the loo.

However …. not infrequently there is a delay. This is through no deliberate fault of the radiotherapists, who are always embarrassed when it happens! This means that this part of the treatment needs a lot of self control, and you end up with bladder management as a seriously needed skill.

I won't go into details, although you might manage to imagine them, but suffice to say that after the radiotherapy session has finished, you end up rushing down the corridor with no shoes and unbuttoned trousers, and in the case of one gent, no trousers at all.

One lady was in such distress (obviously not a prostate disorder) that she cried out, "I'm thoroughly fed up with this water business".

Audible mutterings from other patients, "Right on!", "Hear-hear!", "Tell me about it!"

In the early days I was on the usual learning curve, and hadn't sussed out just how prolonged the effect of drinking more than one litre of water in such a short time can have on the system. What goes in must come out, and the rush to the loo just after treatment doesn't mean that all is accomplished, time to go home in comfort.

It's only the first instalment.

So for the first few days, before I learnt to just wait around for twenty minutes before setting out for home, I found I had to stop (a) at a pub just down the road from the hospital (twice), (b) at a hotel/restaurant in Stokenchurch (always, and we went to eat there several times afterwards as a sort of thank you), (c) on this one and only occasion, at a strangely remote set of toilets on the A40, my route home, not far from the Headington Roundabout on the eastern outskirts of Oxford.

Maria was driving, as I had discovered that somehow my driving had lost focus and concentration, and I thought it crazy to be cured of cancer only to be killed in a road crash.

It was winter, night had fallen, and the loos were remote and set back from the road. The only light was from the busy traffic, and a faint glow from the toilet block.

This type of environment was very familiar to me, and didn't bother me one bit. There was a time when I used to love going out at night, walking in the dark lanes in the countryside around my home town. I found it exhilarating, feeling all my senses on full alert as I found my way along them.

Ok, so I'm crazy, but it was fun!

Back to the A40 loos.

As I stepped out of the car I sensed a dangerous and forbidding atmosphere about the place. The closer I got to the toilet block the stronger it got. As it was dark, and the loos set back from the road, I thought of going to the right hand side of them into some bushes, but it didn't seem to be the right thing to do.

"Lord," I said, "I really need to empty my bladder. I'm in agony."

As I stepped into the toilet block a head appeared around the door of one of the toilets.

I went to do what I came to do and out of the corner of my eye I saw a thick set guy start to move purposefully towards me. Hovering behind him was a smaller man, hanging back a bit, slightly nervous, but beginning to follow.

At the same time a very tall athletic guy came into the toilet block. He paused behind me, looking at the thick set guy. The thick set guy also paused, obviously impressed.

The tall guy came and stood next to me and fumbled with his flies as if he was there for the same reason as me, but he never actually proceeded. In fact I had the clear impression his trousers had no flies!

At first I was a little scared as he seemed about seven foot tall (I'm 5 foot 5 inches so this was a giant!), and especially as I had sensed danger about the place. Then a peace settled over me.

I finished what I came to do, and as I started to move out, so did the very tall guy. He went behind me, and then out of the door, just a step or two ahead of me. The thick set man and his friend had, by this time, retreated behind the door of the toilet.

I looked around to see where the tall guy had gone, but I couldn't see him. The A40 was very busy, and he was so big I should have easily seen him silhouetted by the headlights of the passing traffic as he headed for his car. But there was no-one there, and ours was the only car.

I asked Maria if she had seen him, but she said she hadn't, and no other cars had stopped.

It was then I thought that, surely, this had to be an angel God had sent to protect me. So I thanked Him for His protection in my time of extreme need and vulnerability.

Psalm 91 vv 9,11 *"If you make the Most High your dwelling …. He will command His angels concerning you to guard you in all your ways."*

Chapter 24
THE UNTWISTING OF A STRANGER
(or, How the Crooked became Straight)

Monday 3rd June 2019

I had just been shopping at Lidl in High Wycombe and was walking down Desborough Road. I was feeling thirsty and so went into the newsagents and bought a can of Pepsi-Max. I was feeling a bit of a rebel as Maria keeps telling me I shouldn't drink fizzies; but I think it does you good once in a while. At least that's my theory!

I came out, popped the can, and started to quench my thirst.

Just a few yards ahead of me was a man walking in a most grotesque manner. From his waist up he was almost 90° to the vertical, his left leg stretched out to the side. My heart went out to him, suffering like this.

I came abreast of him and found myself slowing down. I had moved on slightly ahead of him when words came into my head.

"Are you not going to pray for him then?"

I immediately turned, raising my left hand and asked if he would like me to pray for him.

He grabbed my left hand really tightly, and said, "Yes. I'm in such pain."

I replied that I could see that his spine was really twisted, and I raised my right hand and started to pray for him, asking the Holy Spirit to fill him with his love and healing power. I asked Jesus to show His compassion and love by healing him from the pain, and straighten his spine.

Before my eyes he began to straighten up. A look of astonishment came into his face.

He then fell gently back against a hairdresser's shop window, and seemed to shrink. The hairdresser stood up to get a closer look at what was going on.

"You're the man," he said, beginning to find his feet.

"No-no," I said, "it's not me, it's the Holy Spirit and Jesus. They love you."

He came off the window and stood up almost straight.

"You're an angel," he exclaimed in amazement, his eyes wide open.

"No no," I said, "it's not me, it's God, He loves you so much."

He eventually got the message and pointed up to the sky.

"That's right," I said, "It's God. How do you feel?"

"The pain's almost gone. There's hardly any pain left. It's my legs," he went on, "One's longer than the other." So I prayed for God to bring the legs to the same length.

Whether they did, at that moment, I do not know, but I believe God will correct the imbalance in His good time.

We walked along Desborough Road talking, and came to our church building, Kings Church. I told my new friend that if he wanted any more prayer he could call in at our church, pointing it out to him, because they would be so pleased to see him.

I also invited him to come on Sunday. I thought, "Next time I will add – 'and learn about this God who loves you so much that He has healed you'".

When we parted I watched him go, to see how well he was walking. He was walking almost upright and with ease – a different man from the cripple I had met just a few minutes earlier.

This is to the honour of God, who loves each one of us so much, whether we have accepted Him into our lives or not. That is why Jesus came, to call each one of us sinners to follow Him, so that we can find forgiveness, wholeness, and meaning in our lives.

Acts 9 v 34; "Peter said to Aeneas, 'Jesus heals you. Pick up your mat and go home.'"

Chapter 25
THE BIG SENDOFF
(or, Alice's Angels.)

Alice was blind.

Physically that is. But her spirit was 20/20 vision. She was a lovely, gentle, elderly lady.

She came to us because the Convent in Beaconsfield, where she had been taken care of for many years, by very kind nuns, had finally closed.

The Convent where she would have to go from there could not look after her because of the level of care she needed, so the nuns looked for an Old People's Home to continue with her care.

As we were known as a Christian Home, they approached us, and, as we had a room that had just become available, she came to live with us.

She lived with us for many years, and added something special to our Home. She loved singing hymns, and our Home was filled every day with the singing of hymns and spiritual songs, which blessed us all. She felt so much at home with us.

But, finally, she passed away, much to our sorrow.

The church where she wanted her funeral service to be held was St. Michael and All Angels, in Warwick Road, Beaconsfield, just down the road from the model village of Bekonscot. So we, our senior carer, Ruth, and another carer, Elaine, drove over to be at the service.

Not many people were expected, and such it proved. Apart from the vicar who was taking the service, and the funeral directors, only one other person had come.

The service started. The introduction was made, and the entire congregation, all five of us, plus the vicar, stood to sing.

Much to our astonishment the church filled with the sound of a choir singing in four part harmony. Startled, I thought, "More people must have come in at the last minute after all".

I looked over my shoulder and saw ….. the one other person who had come to pay his respects. So who was singing the four part harmony?

Afterwards, we stood outside the church, as the funeral directors whisked Alice's coffin away, and talked about the amazing singing we had just heard.

Ruth, who was not a Christian yet, said, "I think God sent His angels to sing for Alice". I was thinking much the same, and do to this very day.

Wasn't that nice of God?

Psalm 116 verse. *"Precious in the sight of the Lord is the death of His saints."*

ALICE'S POEM

Whilst going through Alice's personal effects we came across this poem, which she must have penned before she went blind.

If I can be still

God will work

His will.

His will is my peace

To release

All quiet security

Of Everlasting Arms

Upholding me.

If I can be still

He will work His will;

Healing all broken things

With the shadow of His wings

And when I am still

And He may work His will,

Though outward things are loud,

And harsh things crowd,

I shall be hidden deep

In the heart of His kind love

Where tired souls sleep.

Chapter 26
THE MIRACLE OF A MOTHER'S SMILE
(or, The Final Miracle.)

Parkinsons!

My mum had Parkinsons disease?

So *that's* the reason why my food had become more flambé than finesse, more scorched than superb, why the times of my evening meal gradually reached eight o'clock from its previously traditional time of six-thirty, and why my mum's smile didn't light up her face any more, as the illness froze her face and denied it any expression. Although it didn't manage to dampen her impish, but kind-hearted, sense of humour!

I didn't notice its gradual take over of my mum's brain until my younger brother returned from University and commented on the change. So off we went to the doctor to see what's wrong, and the diagnosis came with little blue pills to help alleviate the disease. In the 1970s the medication had very unwelcome side effects, which many pills do to this very day, as anyone who takes pills will tell you.

I only heard my mum let us have insight into her struggles twice during the 20 years she endured the illness. They were more in the nature of pieces of information than a complaint; more in the nature of, "Please understand me, this is what I'm struggling with."

The first insight, quite early on, was, "These pills make my food taste like sewage you know". And the second insight was quite late on in those twenty years of facing down the condition with her usual courage, "This illness causes quite a lot of indignity you know".

The pills befuddled her brain a bit, and joined forces with Parkinsons to make her thoughts and her speech slurred and difficult to understand. Unless, that is, she was praying, when her thinking and her words came out with absolute clarity and strength..

Then came the twentieth year of her illness, and Maria and I, with whom she had lived for several years, were sorely in need of a break. We were able to get her into a geriatric hospital in the town for two weeks to enable us to have a holiday.

When we came back, they said two things to us. Firstly, that it was not appropriate for us to take her home, because the level of care needed would be far too much for us to cope with. Secondly, that they were all captivated by my mum's winsomeness and good humour, despite her disabilities.

We visited her often, but eventually she was unable to form the words she wanted to speak. We could see her frustration at no longer being able to talk to us, but there was also a quiet and gracious acceptance of where things were for her.

Several weeks later we had a phone call to say that she was close to the end and could we come. We immediately drove the 2.5 miles to the hospital, but arrived just a few minutes after she died.

Having grieved for her whilst she was alive, because in a way her twenty year illness had already taken her from us, we felt sadness, but it was tinged with relief that she was finally free from her sick body.

The amazing thing was that there was a radiant smile on her face, a face that had been frozen for almost twenty years.

Her eyelids were closed, and I said to Maria, "If her eyes were open, I would say that she had seen the face of Jesus".

"The nurses will have closed the eyelids," she replied. As a trained nurse she knew what the procedure was.

So, in this book, telling of some of the many miracles in my life, this is the final miracle.

The miracle of a mother's smile.

Isaiah 26 v 3; 2 Timothy 4 v 8; "You will keep in perfect peace those whose mind is steadfast, because they trust in you. Now there is in store for me the crown of righteousness which the Lord, the righteous Judge, will award to me."

The following is what I wrote at the time, with the heading I chose.

THE REASON THE SON OF GOD APPEARED …..

(1 John 3 v 8)

I look down at the frail and pitiful body and feel anger well up within me. Why should you be like this? How dare you let that sweet and tender body that shone with love towards me, your son, slowly become crabbed and twisted these twenty painful years; years of creeping indignity where your smile and good humour seem increasingly out of place? And yet, as I look into your eyes I see that the love you have for me, and for your Saviour, glow ever brighter.

Forgive me Lord, for my anger is misplaced. How can I be angry with the victim of Satan? It was he who tempted Eve and Adam to be disobedient to You, and bring a terminal illness upon mankind. Should I not rather be angry at him? Yet I will not berate him, because we too have played our part. And is not justice in Your hands, O Lord God Almighty, and to You and You alone must he answer?

O God, my Lord, You are a wonderful and merciful God, because over all her suffering is the shadow of Your mercy, the cross of Jesus Christ. There is the final miracle where Jesus destroyed the works of the evil one. Beneath the suffering and pain of body and mind lies the peace of forgiveness, and the joy of knowing You, her Lord and her Redeemer.

Thank You Lord that You have decreed that because she has decided to be Your child the final word is Yours, and, therefore, You have said that though this broken defeated body will die, she herself will rise victorious at the resurrection in a new and wonderful body. A body that You will give her, that will be totally beyond anything we could imagine or wish for, a body that will never know suffering and pain. And I too will one day join with her in praising Your Name for ever, and for ever.

1 John Ch. 3 v 8. The reason the Son of God appeared was to destroy the devil's work.

Chapter 27
AFTERWORD

Well, that's it then.

You will probably realise that being a Christian doesn't guarantee a trouble free life, and you'd be right. In fact life can be a lot harder than it would otherwise be, but the ending is better, and lasts for ever.

I don't pretend that all my aches and pains have been miraculously healed, they haven't, and, there are times when we have to live with the consequences of bad decisions.

However, there is one thing to remember, which is, that even when we make bad decisions, God can bring some good out of them when we ask His forgiveness, especially if we ask Him to bring good out of it. He will also help us turn over a new leaf and lead a better sort of life, one that follows His leading, and His values.

Of course, I have had good times as well. I've enjoyed being a husband, a dad, and a granddad. I've loved singing, and acting, and making loaves of bread.

I had an allotment for many years, which was hard work, but it was great to experiment with sowing different types of carrot, runner beans, leeks, and so on; and had the great joy of carrying the resulting crops home to feed the family.

I have been refreshed by holidays at the seaside, exhilarated by gazing out at snow covered mountains from the top of Ben Macdhui, entranced by the view from the top of a heart stimulating hike up Snowdon, camped by woodland and river, and heard sheep munching breakfast bread from our invaded rucksacks. I have enjoyed the irresistible smell of bacon frying over an open wood fire, (which they don't like you doing these days - make wood fires I mean, not fry bacon!), cleansed by bathing in a freezing-cold moorland stream - which left me wonderfully allaglow - and walked with camping gear on my back until my legs seem to belong to themselves and not to me (well ….. maybe, with that one, it's the memory that's fun!!).

I've appreciated having good friends, a loving family, and good neighbours to get on with. Actually the list seems to go on and on, so maybe I will stop there.

However, when all is said and done, the really important point of my life is accepting Jesus as Lord of my life, confessing to Him when I am sinful and need His forgiveness, asking for it, accepting it, and wanting to live in a way that pleases Him.

Jesus wants us to have a relationship with Him, not a religion about Him. That is the reason why He came down to earth.

We all of us, every one of us, has a rebellious nature that has broken the relationship between ourselves and God.

The Good News is, God loves each and every one of us so much that His Love compelled Him to do something about restoring the relationship between Him and us.

That is why Jesus came down to earth by being born like one of us, lived like we do, then allowed Himself to be crucified. It is why He died on the Roman cross they nailed Him to. First He was flogged with forty lashes, the bits of metal and bone on the lash tearing pieces out of His body. Weakened by the loss of His flesh, and losing blood, He no longer had the strength to carry the cross to which they were to nail Him.

Asphyxiated, Jesus' body died, the result, and intention, of crucifixion.

His death was made certain by a Roman soldier, who, using his training, experience, and expertise, thrust his spear straight into Jesus heart, releasing blood, and blood plasma, which separate from each other following death. He was, indeed, dead.

From the third day after He died, Jesus was seen by, and spoke to, many hundreds of people. He had indeed risen from the dead.

His love for us drove Him to do this, because separation from Him means that when our body dies, our spirit goes where He is not, and that is more awful than any distressing thing we have ever experienced during our life on this earth; but living with Him will be pure joy and peace. *(See "The Watery Grave", and "Steps to Heaven".)*

That is why Jesus calls people today to follow Him. However, the choice is always ours.

Make no mistake; we are all in the same boat. We have all done wrong things, and need God's forgiveness – no exception. And forgiveness is what God offers. But we have to find forgiveness the way God has decided, and not a way we, maybe influenced by others, have decided we want to believe.

It is so important to realise that we have sinned against God, and that we have to ask for His forgiveness. We also have to accept God's authority over our lives. In effect we have to make Him Lord of our lives, and allow the Holy Spirit of God to guide and strengthen us to live a better way of life.

God meets us where we are, but doesn't want us to stay there. If you fell into a pit with a lot of mud at the bottom, and someone rescued you, you would like to have a nice shower and get rid of all the mud wouldn't you! To God, our sins are very much like the mud, and He wants to clean us up, and show us how to stop falling into muddy pits and getting messed up again. That's a lifetime's work! But He is patient with us.

Some people accept Him as Lord of their lives and others just won't. We are, of course, all free to choose, and, as you know, every choice has its consequences, good or bad.

Note that we are souls with earthly bodies, not bodies with souls. Those people who don't make Jesus Lord of their life have voted not to live with Him for ever.

The only way we get a new body after this one has died is to live with Jesus for ever. If you vote not to make Jesus Lord of your life, you just don't get a new body after this earthly one has died. Your spirit will be conscious, but not able to feel, see, smell, taste, hear, or touch. It doesn't end, nor can you escape from it. What do you think that is going to be like?

So, if you haven't made a choice yet, what are you going to decide? To me this is a "no-brainer". By the way, to make no choice means you don't accept Jesus as Lord, with all its awful consequences.

God's heart aches for you to accept Him into your life and live in joy and peace.

How about reading "Steps to Heaven" and "The Watery Grave" once again?

And so, it's over to you. As always, it's your choice.

Hebrews Ch.9 v 27 *"Man is destined to die once, and after that to face judgement."*

Some more verses from The Bible; God speaking to us.

"For God loved the world so much that He sent His one and only son, (Jesus), that whoever believes in Him will not perish but have life that never ends. Whoever believes in Him is not condemned, but whoever does not believe in Him is condemned already because he has not believed in God's one and only Son."

John Ch. 3 vv 16 &18

"If we claim we do not sin, we deceive ourselves and His Truth is not in us. If we confess our sins, He is faithful and just and will forgive us our sins, and cleanse us from all unrighteousness."

1 John Ch. 1 vv 8 &9

"But because of His great love for us, God, Who is rich in mercy, made us alive with Christ even when we were dead in our sins – it is by God's grace you have been saved."

Ephesians Ch. 2 vv 4 &5.

"Jesus said to those who put their trust in Him, 'In my Father's house there are many rooms. I am going there to prepare a place for you. I will come back and take you to be with me that you also may be where I am'."

John Ch. 14 vv 2 &3

"The thief hanging on the cross next to Him said, 'Jesus, remember me when you come into your kingdom'. Jesus answered, 'I tell you the truth, today you will be with me in Paradise'."

Luke Ch.23 vv 42 &43

Remember the short story on page 127...

Chapter 28

MY TESTIMONY OF GOD'S FAITHFULNESS TO HIS PROMISES TO ME, IN WALKING WITH ME THROUGH THE GOOD TIMES AND THE CHALLENGING TIMES

(Given to my guests at the celebration of my 75ᵗʰ Birthday at Wrights Meadow Community Centre, High Wycombe, Bucks.)

I was born towards the end of the Second World War, and, therefore, today, I am celebrating 75 years of life. So, what has my 75 years of life amounted to?

It caused me to reflect on the following questions.

What has been the major influence on my life? Has my life amounted to anything worthwhile? Has there been purpose in my life? Or has it all been a waste of time?

Some, like Richard Dawkins and friends, would seek to persuade us that this human race to which we all belong, is just an accident of myriad co-incidences, and our lives are just flotsam and jetsam which appear for a moment in the eons of time, and then disappear without trace forever.

I can see why so many people become seriously depressed with this philosophy of life, if you can describe it as "life", and why so many long for something that re-assures them of their intrinsic worth and personal value. What I eventually came to realise as "I am valid". By that I mean my physical appearance, my natural abilities, and those abilities that I lack. The acceptance that, "I am valid as I am," with all my shortcomings and odd ways of going about life.

For instance, my wife Maria and I often approach a similar job or situation in ways that differ from each other, but both ways can be valid. We are just wired differently, and that can so often be a strength when making decisions.

So what of my life?

What has come across to me most strongly is God's faithfulness to me in every circumstance of my life, throughout the good times and the challenging times. The following gives you a bird's eye view of God's involvement in my life over the last ¾ of a century. (And wow, yes, that does sound a long time!)

Let's start at age 9.

I was a proper little atheist. I didn't need to write a book, like some have done, to tell you why, because it was so simple. I couldn't see God, couldn't touch God, couldn't smell God, couldn't hear God, and couldn't taste God.

Conclusion, He couldn't exist.

Then someone came to our Sunday School and described hell, and it sounded like a place to avoid putting on your holiday list. Then he described Heaven, and this sounded like a brilliant place to spend your holidays.

Then he told us that Jesus came to die for us, so that, if we accepted Him as Lord of our lives, then we would be forgiven all our sins, and, we wouldn't go to hell. That sounded like a really bright idea.

Jesus was also raised from the dead three days after He died on the cross, and so we would live with this amazing man days without end.

I still wasn't convinced God existed, but avoiding hell seemed to be a no-brainer! So I said, "God, if you really do exist, make me walk home on air like this man said. If you exist I really mean it when I say I will make you Lord of my life, and I will follow you forever."

So, a short time later there I was walking down Pipers Hill Road in Kettering, and I couldn't feel the pavement under my feet! I seemed to be travelling as high as the lampposts. It was amazing! Fantastic stuff! I felt so exhilarated! Then I saw a man walking up on the other side of the road.

"Oh gosh," I thought, "What is he going to think if he sees me up here?"

But he didn't look up. He was too busy looking across the road with a slightly puzzled and thoughtful look on his face.

Many years later I learnt that others have walked on air when they have accepted Jesus as Lord of their lives, which was slightly disappointing, as I'd thought it to be such a unique thing. But at the same time I felt encouraged, as I saw that God gives all of us proofs of His reality, sometimes in similarly spectacular ways.

Roll on seven years to 16 years old.

Our church, Fuller Baptist Church in Kettering, had regular full-immersion baptisms, and I quite liked the excitement of people committing themselves to God.

Then it was my call!

I was standing there on the balcony, with the minister saying, "Those who want to be baptised, come forward to the front."

Well, I was a desperately shy teenager, and could not see myself going forward in front of 300 or so people. But a pressure began to build up inside me to go out to be baptised. I knew it was God calling me.

Eventually I said, "God, I'll go out afterwards".

Immediately two pictures came into my mind.

On the left was a deep black pit, with wisps of transparent beings moving around. Each had a downturned mouth, and though there was no sound, I could sense the misery, and the desperate desolation.

I had an affirmation of that desolation many years later when emerging from a dream. I think God had taken me to see once again the awfulness of hell, and this time the sense of desolation was much stronger, even though it was fading away.

It was the most desperately awful sight; beyond anything you could imagine. There are no words to express what it was like. How I wanted my non-Christian friends to come to know the freedom from hell we have in Jesus. How I started to talk to them more purposefully about God's love for them, and His longing for them to know Him, and find freedom in Him, and a future with Him.

So that black pit was where the path of disobedience led.

On the right was a time-line of my life. Like the town of High Wycombe, where I lived for over forty years, and Buckingham, where I now live, there were steep hills and deep valleys. The hills were the challenges of life, and the valleys were the peaceful days when life was a little easier. There were several hills and valleys, and words came into my mind, "But I will be with you".

Wind on to age 21, and a few months after my dad had died, which was a big shock to me. I was at a mid-week prayer meeting with my mother waiting for it to start, and behind us I heard a couple talking about an elderly man who had passed away in the prayer meeting just a couple of weeks before.

I thought, "That must have been amazing; praying to God one second, and the next you are talking to Him face to face!"

Suddenly, I was there! I was walking up a flight of broad steps towards two golden gates, which were flung wide open. Two angels, one each side of the gates, holding on to the gate post with one hand and the other reaching down to me, with huge welcoming smiles on their faces.

Between the gateposts shone out the most beautiful light I had ever seen, and a hubbub of happy, joyful voices talking excitedly with one another.

A voice came into my mind, "You can come in if you want Alan".

I sensed though, from its slightly reserved tone, that it wouldn't be the best choice, but He would allow it.

"My mother!" Concern flashed into my mind.

Losing a husband was bad, but a son as well so soon afterwards? That would be devastating.

Immediately I was back in the prayer room, and a great fear welled up within me. I had just seen the beauty, love, joy, peace and safety of God's presence, and I was back in a world of self-centredness, evil, fear, and discontent.

Wind on again, to forty years old, and I contracted Labarynthitis.

This is an infection of the middle ear, which causes nausea at the most trifling movement. I thought this was it, I was dying! I was fed air-sickness pills, and for three months I learnt to cope with being as motionless as it is possible to be.

It turned out to be the best time of my life so far!

God was true to His promise, and I could feel the love and peace of His presence with me during the tricky three months it took me to recover.

In 1983 Maria and I set up a small Old Peoples' Home. It was great, and I enjoyed the 15 caps I wore, from bookkeeper, project manager, staff trainer, odd job man, entertainer, carpet and loo cleaner – that's when it got really messy!

In 1994 I was visiting an international charity on some errand or other, and the person I was told to meet gave me one look and asked me to complete a questionnaire. He explained that it was a stress questionnaire that his organisation gave to people returning from extended spells of working abroad in difficult situations.

I scored 9 out of 10! The higher the score the greater the stress level.

The recommendation was to stop work for three months and take a relaxing break. However, this would have meant employing someone to do what I was doing, and we could not afford it. So I had to soldier on.

It took us ten years to sell the home.

In 2004, when we finally handed it over to the people who had bought it from us, I realised I could not remember what had happened during the previous two years.

It was a total blank.

But the words came into my mind, "I can rebuild you Alan".

Roll forward twelve years and it is 2016. I had been experiencing a drop off of energy over several years, but thought it was the result of getting more elderly. Then, in late July, I realised that my energy had dropped rapidly in just three months.

I took a blood test and found my PSA was 96.

Further tests showed my prostate riddled with cancer, and my Gleeson Score was 9 out of 10 – yes, that's bad, really bad.

The day before I went for my radiotherapy at the Churchill Oxford University Hospital, I said to God, "Is this my home-call, or do you want me here for a bit longer".

The next day I was reading in Isaiah, and suddenly it was like someone nudged me and said, 'read that again'. So I went back several verses and read it again.

The sense of it was, "You are my servant. I will defeat your enemy. You will look for him and not find him".

And so it proved. At the time of writing my last PSA reading was 0.28 – yes, that's good, very good.

Everyone has trials in life, or if you don't you are very fortunate. Through them all I have found God to be at my side, encouraging me, and walking through the pain, discomfort, challenges, and disappointments.

God has also been with me through the good times, whilst enjoying the beauty of His creation, the intimacy with Maria and the life we have lived together, the two wonderful sons we have, their wives and children (our grandchildren), my wider British family, and the amazing Cypriot family I married into.

I love the wonder of God's Church, the Christian church, with people from around 50 different nationalities and cultures worshipping God together in the church community we belonged to in High Wycombe for 25 years. A Christian community that loves, supports, and respects one another, all brought together and united under the Headship of Jesus; a community that glories in the richness that results from our unity in diversity. Yes there are challenges, and we embrace them, and learn from them.

Through all of my life God has always been faithful to me, even though I may not have always been faithful to Him and His ways. When I sincerely ask for forgiveness and ask Him to change me, my whole being fills up with His Peace, and the warmth and tenderness of His Love.

I commend Him to you. God, Creator of the Universe and all that is in it, Who is Father, Son (i.e. Jesus**), and Holy Spirit, all three in one God, from everlasting to everlasting.

Yes, I commend this amazing God to you. Don't miss out.

Ask Him to be Lord of your life - today. Amen.

Alan D Edmondson

Granddad, Husband, Dad,

Brother

Cousin, Brother-in-law and relative of many other sorts

**

Incidentally, Jesus didn't start His existence as a baby born of a young woman called Mary in a stable in Bethlehem.

That was when He came down to earth in the form of a human being.

God tells us that Jesus existed before the creation of the world. In fact the world was created by Jesus and for Him.

Check it out by reading John Chapter 1, and there are other passages as well that you can look up, such as:

Colossians Ch. 1 vv 9-20

Philippians Ch. 2 vv 5-11

And there are many others.

I suggest you also read the fast paced 'Life of Jesus' written by Mark, found in the New Testament of the Holy Bible.

"Those who are wise will take all this to heart;
they will see in our history
the faithful Love of the Lord."
Psalm 107 verse 43 (NLT)

THE CHOICE

A short story

(in which you choose your own ending)

Please note: unlike the preceding stories, the following is a fictional story, and any resemblance to anyone living or dead is entirely coincidental.

Kevin stood motionless, shoulders slumped, hat limp at his side. Dark brown hair flecked with grey hung like curled and pointed tails about his forehead, and the drenching rain mingled with his tears as if the whole of heaven could see his heart and wept.

His dulled eyes watched the puddles form on the freshly turned brown-black earth. Such a tiny mound, such a ridiculously small resting place for the life that had so hugely filled his own.

The church clock chimed seven o'clock, and his head jerked up, the muscles of his face tightening with rage. He raised his fist, white knuckled, to the soaring steeple.

"Call yourself a loving God! He was only three!" His voice rose in a crescendo. "Why? Why? Why?"

Sudden pain gripped his stomach and he doubled over, his voice a whisper, "He was such a happy child. So very happy."

He lived it all once again, the little hand squirming out of his own, the joyful cry of "Mummy!", the fear and helplessness as Jamie disappeared amongst the wheels; the squeal of tyres, the smell of burnt rubber, the drivers' ashen faces aghast, the broken child like a bloodied bundle of clothes thrown aside, a dead child, his child, his only child, and the crushing guilt, the anger.

And now the tears. Thank God for the tears, hidden in the rain.

The soft clunk of a heavy door made him look up. A light appeared through the stained glass of the rose window over the door of the church. The rain stopped suddenly and a stray shaft of sunlight broke through the gathering gloom and brought to life the saints around the porch as if kissed by the love of heaven.

Subconsciously drawn by the light Kevin found himself walking to the porch, and, as the sunlight dimmed and died, he grasped the wrought-iron ring-handle and pushed hard to open the heavy nail-studded oak door. It opened slowly into the subdued lighting of the church.

Church! How rarely had he crossed that threshold. What was this really all about? He knew so little. A God of Love Father Stephen said on those rare occasions he had come.

Kevin walked to the top of the nave and looked down toward the altar. The main lights had been turned off. Dimly he could see the grey-white of the limestone pillars soaring into the darkness of the roof, and in front of each he could just make out the statue of a saint. At the front, to the left, Father Stephen had lit a candle in front of St. Anselm, from whom the church took its name, and was kneeling, praying, his hands resting on a chair in front of him.

The two candles by the altar were also burning, and lit up a large wooden cross hung suspended above it, with Jesus crucified upon it. Black nail heads were painted on the wrists and the crossed feet, and a trail of blood ran down each arm to the elbow. Another trail of blood flowed from the feet to the foot of the cross, joining the blood pouring from a wide wound just under his ribs. On his head was a crown plaited from thorny twigs, and more blood.

Kevin crossed himself instinctively. It was a while since he had done that! Not since Jamie was baptised. And now .....

He walked quietly to where Father Stephen knelt and looked down at the old man at his prayers. So focused, so peaceful, so .... But what did he know of pain, of the loss of a precious child? For that matter what did God know of pain, hidden in His heaven a million miles away from reality, remote from human suffering? What does He care? Can you hear me God?

Kevin cleared his throat and Father Stephen look up. The candlelight gleamed off this snow-white hair.

"Kevin!"

The priest's face broke into a broad smile deepening the creases of old age, and then looked solemn.

"I'm so glad you came .... and so soon after the funeral too."

He looked searchingly into Kevin's eyes.

"It's a difficult time for you. It must be hard, so very very hard."

He place his big hands on the bench in front of him. Kevin noticed for the first time the swollen joints and the twisted fingers.

Father Stephen slowly bent his right leg. He pushed down with hands and leg, lips pressed together, determined. He rose slowly. Half way there was a crack, and then another. Kevin winced. Father Stephen's expression did not change. Kevin willed him to stand, and at last he stood, teetered for a moment and then sat on the bench by his side, breathing deeply, breathless.

"Excuse me sitting down, Kevin, won't you? After I've been kneeling I don't seem to be able to keep my balance like I used to, not for a while anyway."

He fiddled clumsily at his right ear, adjusting his hearing aid.

"Is there anything I can do to help?"

"Ask God to give me back my Jamie, perhaps?"

The words came out sarcastically.

He paused.

"Why did God let it happen, Father?" His voice rose. "Don't you tell us He loves us? Look what this loving God has allowed to happen to me!"

Kevin's voice rang around the rafters, and he suddenly felt ashamed.

"I'm sorry."

Father Stephen reached out and touched his arm, and spoke gently.

"That's alright my son. God can cope with your anger. He understands your pain."

"What! Up there in His heaven? How can He? How can He possibly know? I've lost a son, remember? When did He go through that pain?"

There was a pause, and then the words came, almost soundlessly, and hung in the air, alive.

"About two thousand years ago. Remember? Jesus' pain was not just physical as He hung there on the cross, but the even more excruciating pain of separation from The Father. And The Father felt the same excruciating pain of separation from His one and only Son, Jesus."

A breath of air touched Kevin's forehead and he looked up. He could almost see drops of blood dripping off the foot of the cross onto the floor of the church. The bloodied face of the crucified Jesus shone in the candlelight, and His eyes seemed to be looking into his eyes, looking into his very soul, pleading with him.

"Evil men took Him and murdered Him because they thought He was a threat to their authority, to their religion, and to the money in their pocket. What He was actually doing was showing them God Himself."

Kevin felt a shiver pass up his spine. Shaking off the gaze he turned to look intently at the old priest.

"Evil thought it had won, Kevin. But in reality love had won. Because, you know, love does not compromise, even in the face of death."

A misty look came over the old man's eyes. He put his hands on the seat each side of him, leaned forward and started to push himself upwards. Standing at last he held on to the back of the chair to steady himself. His false teeth had become dislodged with the effort and he gently pushed them back into place.

"He knew what He was doing you know."

"What?"

"Jesus. He knew what He was doing."

"What do you mean?" Kevin felt lost.

"Dying on a cross, in so much pain."

Father Stephen turned to look at the cross over the altar. Kevin followed his gaze. Those eyes. How can they look so alive, so full of .... love?

"He knew this was what He had to do one day. That this was why He was born."

"To die .... Like this?"

"Yes."

Kevin felt like he'd missed something.

"How can someone be born to die .... so violently? What would it achieve?"

"Have you never sworn at anyone Kevin?"

"What?"

"Have you never wanted to get your own back, never stolen a piece of paper from your employer? Have you never told a lie to avoid getting blamed for something you'd done?"

Kevin shrugged, embarrassed.

"I'm only human."

"Exactly."

What on earth is this old man getting at?

"You see, Kevin, such things make us imperfect. We are all 'only human'."

He gave a wan smile. "Even an old priest like me who everyone thinks is holy."

"Well, no-one's perfect."

131

"So do you think God can let something imperfect spoil His perfect Heaven, Kevin? Let me in to spoil it? Let anyone of us in to spoil it?"

"I had hoped that Jamie might at least….," Kevin's voice trailed off.

"Oh yes! Jamie *is* alright. There is a way for us to get into heaven. Only one. We have to choose to go that way and Jamie chose it."

"What are you talking about?"

Father Stephen made a faint gesture with his left hand.

"The cross! You see, if Jesus hadn't died all of us humans would have to die. Every last one of us. And no, there would be no hope, and yes, I wouldn't be a priest."

The beeswax candles, these made with old fashioned wicks, burned brighter as the wicks grew long, and Kevin looked once more up to the cross and into the face of Jesus. The eyes held his gaze as Father Stephen continued,

"But Jesus' death gives us hope of heaven. You see, the hardest bit was not the nails and the suffocation but what *you* know Kevin. The pain of separation from a loved one. Do you remember? Jesus cried out, 'My God! My God! Why have You forsaken me?' Do you remember that from our Easter reading?"

Kevin nodded. "Yes."

He felt confused as questions and conflicting emotions rushed around in his head. Does God feel pain? But I know *I* feel pain. I've lost the only son I've ever had.

And then words from the Bible, so often read, so often not understood, came streaming into his mind, 'For God so loved the world that He gave His only Son'.

God had only one Son? And He died too? Violently? Like my little Jamie? My precious Jamie?

The old priest was speaking again.

"You see, Kevin, it's our imperfections, the seemingly little things, what we call sin, that separate us from God, that disqualify us from His perfect heaven."

"So what *does* it qualify us for?" Kevin was feeling truculent.

"A permanent separation from the perfect love God has for us."

Father Stephen looked at the grey stone flags of the nave and heaved a sigh.

"What we call Hell."

Kevin looked at the crown of snow white hair, suddenly fascinated, knowing there was more. The hair moved and became a smiling face, and words gushed out from the old priest's lips.

"The good news is that God loves us so much that He doesn't leave us to sort it out for ourselves, He knew we can't. He loves us so much, He wants to forgive us, but justice has to be done. Someone has to pay the penalty for our sinful ways."

Kevin felt horrified, incredulous.

"Are you saying that God let His Son die .. like this ..," he gestured at the cross, "without trying to do something to save Him? I'd have saved Jamie if I could," his voice rose angrily to choke back his sobs,"… but I was too late … it happened all too quickly. What sort of God is that?" His voice ended in a shout.

Father Stephen stood motionless regarding him for a moment, and then said, so gently, that the words caressed Kevin's ears like balm.

"It would be cruel Kevin, and so it was. But you see, Father and Son planned it together. To save the likes of you and me from eternal suffering. Jesus agreed to suffer instead. Not just the physical and mental torture of being nailed to a cross, but the emotional pain of being separated from one another. It was a two way thing, Kevin. Each separated for a time from the One they loved more than anything else in the whole of space and time." He paused. "You see, Jesus, is God Himself. The God who said sin must be punished allowed Himself to be punished instead. He gave sentence of death on Himself so that we would not need to be punished."

"I find that hard to believe."

"And that is the crux of the whole thing. For it to work, you have to believe it's true. It doesn't apply automatically. You have to choose to believe it. No-one can choose for you."

"How can I believe in such a thing?" Kevin felt desperate. Wanting to believe, struggling to break through his doubts. What was it someone said to him once? Doubt your doubts?

"It's a funny thing. I found it hard to believe it as well. But I wanted to believe it was true, not really being sure, not really believing it. But, strange you know, once I said I believed, it was like a fog rolled away, and it seemed so obviously true."

Kevin shook his head. The priest's voice came tenderly.

"Jamie believed it you know. With the simplicity of a child who can see the truth. He told me many a time that he loved Jesus. He's now with God in His heaven. You could join him again someday you know."

Kevin looked at him, then at the figure on the cross. The old fashioned candle wicks were in need of trimming, and the light was growing dim, but still the eyes held his gaze, pleading with him.

"I'm not sure I want to believe." His voice rose, "This loving God let my son die."

"And he let my brother die too."

Kevin's eyes opened wide in amazement.

"What?"

"He died in my arms. We were pilots in the same squadron." He looked into Kevin's eyes. "It was 1944, June 7th. He'd been badly shot up after a raid. He made it home, and I dragged him out of his cockpit to carry him to the ambulance. He died right there, in my arms. "Was I angry with God!"

The priest reached for a small bible on the table in front of Saint Anselm. For the first time Kevin saw that in the centre the cover was torn – a hole. Fingers swollen with arthritis fumbled at the cover and eventually managed to fold it back.

"See?"

Kevin saw a piece of dull jagged metal about the size of a ten pence piece.

"I nearly bought it as well." He smiled. "You could say that the Word of God saved me. It was in my shirt pocket, and it stopped the shrapnel. And the Word of God does save us. From eternal separation from God. Which is hell. You just have to believe it and act on it. As for my anger, I realised that it's unreal to think that this life can have no pain. Just look around you. It's full of tragedy. But it's not God who causes it. It's men and women. That's why Jesus had to come. Why He died. To buy us a life after this one that is free from these things."

"A dead man brings us life?"

"Oh no! He's not dead. Not now. God brought Him back to life again. If He hadn't how could we believe that we can have another life? And your Jamie is living another life right now. He loves Jesus. And you can too."

Father Stephen's voice became more urgent.

"Just believe it and act on it Kevin."

Kevin looked into his eyes and suddenly admired this old man with his snow white hair, his arthritis, his hearing aid and false teeth, his memories of a dying brother, his faith in an Almighty God who loves us so much that He gave up an only Son so that we might have life for ever in His heaven.

But it didn't make sense.

"Does it have to make sense?" The words seemed to drop into Kevin's mind from another world. He looked up, startled.

"What?"

"I said, just believe it and act on it Kevin. Then it will make sense."

He felt confused. Those weren't the words that had just dropped into his mind.

"How can I believe something that doesn't make any sense to me?"

Again, words dropped into his mind.

"Why does it have to make sense? It just has to be true doesn't it? Do you have to know everything before you trust it and use it? Do you have to make sense of fuel technology before you fill your car with petrol? Or do you just trust in the truth that it will make your car work?"

Kevin felt a shiver down his spine. The old man's lips hadn't moved.

"But you let my son die. You let my son die. Didn't you let my son die?"

"Kevin, believe it." Father Stephen's voice was urgent, vibrant. "Embrace it Kevin. Jesus said He is the light of the world. Embrace the light Kevin, for the only alternative is darkness. For ever! It never ends."

"My little boy died. My Jamie. How could He have let him die? A God of Love? Don't make me laugh!"

"Kevin, my son ... "

"Get lost! I will never, ever, forgive Him."

The candle by the altar guttered, and the cross disappeared into the darkness.

Damned priest! What does he know?

Kevin stamped across the cold grey slabs and pulled at the heavy door. It was as if it did not want to let him go, to hold him there to hear more, to give him a chance to change his mind.

ALTERNATIVE ENDING 1.

Anger gave him strength, and overcame the stubbornness of the door. It squeaked open, a mournful grieving sound. He stepped through into the porch and looked back.

Father Stephen had trimmed and relit the candle by the cross, and was already kneeling, praying, his hair shining like spun silver in the light from the candle, creating a halo around his head.

Kevin watched as the oak door swung slowly back on its black hinges, gradually cutting out the light. The soft clang as it latched itself sent a shudder down his spine. Something final seemed to have taken place.

Rain ran down the church windows and dripped off the sills, unseen tears in the blackness of the world. A gust of wind drove icy spikes of rain into Kevin's eyes and effortlessly chilled his heart.

With a last look at the now closed door, Kevin adjusted his hat, turned up his coat collar, and stepped out into the darkness.

ALTERNATIVE ENDING 2.

Kevin paused in his struggle and looked back. Father Stephen had trimmed and relit the candle by the cross, and was already kneeling, praying, his hair shining like spun silver in the light from the candle, creating a halo around his head. The new and brighter candlelight lit up the image of Jesus with a fresh intensity. His arms, opened wide on the cross, took on a new meaning, arms open in welcome to all who would come to Him. More words dropped into his mind.

"Come to Me, Kevin. Just come to Me. Find Peace and release of your pain from Me. I know what you are going through. Just come to Me."

Kevin found himself drawn back down the nave towards the cross, the image of Jesus, and the praying elderly priest. Kevin knelt down beside the priest and placed his left arm gently around his bowed shoulders. Father Stephen raised his eyes, brimful with tears, enquiringly. Their eyes met in mutual grief and understanding. Without a word being spoken, tears began to fall, warm tears, healing tears, tears gratefully shed.

"I will believe, Father, I will believe."

The old priest looked earnestly into Kevin's eyes.

"Then confess your sins to him."

"Father, tell me what to say. I don't know what to say."

"Say, 'Jesus, please forgive me my sins'".

"Jesus, please forgive me my sins."

"Thank You for dying on the cross for me."

"Thank You for dying on the cross for me."

"In Your mercy count my sins amongst those you took upon Yourself on the cross."

And Kevin continued to repeat all that Father Stephen asked him to pray.

"I renounce Satan and all his ways", "Jesus I make You Lord of my life", "Holy Spirit come and fill me with Yourself, and direct my life to live as God wants me to live", "I am now yours", "Amen".

And suddenly Kevin did understand. It was as if the dark clouds had lifted and the sun had shone into his soul.

In his head echoed words from one of the few sermons he had heard Father Stephen preach; that Jesus had said, "I am the light of the world. Those who believe in me will never die, but receive eternal life."

"Father Stephen, I *do* believe."

And Kevin bowed his head in thankful worship.

The old priest smiled, and the angels sang.

Well, that's the story. Which ending would you like to have? And having chosen, does that tell you anything about yourself? Furthermore, does it indicate something you need to do?

AND FINALLY ………

When we see our weakness
And turn to God

When we turn our back on foolishness
And embrace wisdom

We are transformed from childishness
To maturity

We move from fragility
To strength

From the image of Adam
Towards the image of God.

Michael J Edmondson
(Used with permission)
(21/06/2020)

9 781911 697718